LEAP
FROG

Celebrating 35 Years of
Penguin Random House India

'A must-read for professionals and entrepreneurs from all backgrounds. Mukesh Sud and Priyank Narayan have succinctly encapsulated the six fundamentals needed to thrive in any career. Exciting gyaan, intelligibly packaged from IIMA and Ashoka'.

—**Sanjeev Bikhchandani, Founder, Naukri.com;**
Founder and Trustee, Ashoka University

'*Leapfrog* is most relevant in today's context. It offers some of the finest academic research in a practical, real-world framework. This witty and engaging book should be part of every young professional's library'.

—**Ashish Dhawan, Founding Chairperson,**
Ashoka University; Board Member,
Bill and Melinda Gates Foundation

'Mukesh and Priyank dig deep and offer brilliant insights into the challenges of professional and personal growth. Their anecdotal style of writing is a reflection of the conversations they create in the classroom, supporting each story with evidence-based research. *Leapfrog* is a powerful book for everyone who cares about thriving in their career'.

—**Pramath Raj Sinha, Chairperson,**
Board of Trustees, Ashoka University;
Founding Dean, Indian School of Business

'In this uncertain and complex world, it is reassuring to have a robust framework to leapfrog ahead. Mukesh Sud and Priyank Narayan offer such an elegantly synthesized set of practices reflecting the current state of the art with wonderful stories and examples'.

—**Rishikesha T. Krishnan,**
Director and Professor of Strategy,
Indian Institute of Management Bangalore

'A delightful feature of Professors Sud and Narayan's book is that the ideas it espouses are also applied in the writing of the book. *Leapfrog* solves the problem of how to get the reader to reconsider their approach to challenges at work and in life. Through engaging stories, backed by extensive research, *Leapfrog* presents practical principles and practices for the reader to bring awareness and a deliberate approach to the problems they face. The read is fun, thought-provoking and will inspire you to thrive'.

—Aleksandar Pilipovic,
Managing Director, Goldman Sachs

'*Leapfrog*, written by Mukesh and Priyank, uses robust research to provide practical advice to anyone who wishes to grow and thrive. The conversational style of writing and lovely illustrations will be a delight to all readers'.

—Neharika Vohra, Vice Chancellor,
Delhi Skill and Entrepreneurship University

'Mukesh and Priyank come with incredible insights from classrooms in two of the leading institutions in the country. Don't miss this opportunity to peek inside their class and join the conversation with their students'.

—Varun Berry, Managing Director,
Britannia Industries Ltd

'Practical ideas for entrepreneurial success, supported by evidence-based multidisciplinary research. A must-read for all budding professionals out there'.

—Himanshu Rai, Director,
Indian Institute of Management Indore

'We live in unprecedented times. In this age of uncertainty, it is impossible to ascertain the appropriateness of an option to follow and often to enumerate the set of potential options. It is best then to experiment with actions and this book provides a toolkit for envisioning possible futures and identifying promising moves by which to navigate one's future. It is sure to give the reader some aha moments'.

—Errol D'Souza, Director,
Indian Institute of Management Ahmedabad

'With pragmatic ideas for a thriving career, Mukesh and Priyank have managed to emphatically articulate a framework for success at work. A must-read for aspiring professionals'.

—Aditya Ghosh, Co-Founder, Akasa Air;
Former President, Indigo Airlines

'A must for all entrepreneurs and those seeking to become entrepreneurs. It will help understand a basic mindset to start a business, covering areas that are otherwise learned by trial and error. As academics, the authors have also skilfully leveraged their entrepreneurial background and years of experience to ensure actionable insights. The numerous real-world examples bring their theories to life in a way that is easy to read, comprehend, and apply. Entrepreneurial thinking can also be applied to planning your career. Today with the sheer breadth of options available, entrepreneurial thinking is a necessity. As an entrepreneur myself, I have rarely come across a book that so seamlessly combines relevant academic insights with real-world practitioners' experience of entrepreneurship'.

—**Abhinaya Chaudhari, Co-Founder,**
Big Basket and LaundryMate

'Intellectually stimulating and a lucid read, *Leapfrog* is a methodological checklist for thriving in life'.

—**Deep Kalra, Founder and Chairman, MakeMyTrip**

'The six practices and pillars that Mukesh and Priyank have described are so apt in this rapidly changing world. I can imagine students, young professionals and seasoned executives all benefiting from these simple principles. What makes it very easy to understand and absorb is the story-telling style that ensures you latch on to every word. This book has the makings of a masterpiece that originates from India'.

—**Srikant Sastri, President, TiE Delhi-NCR;**
Chairman, IIM Calcutta Innovation Park

'An amazing insight into what it takes to sustain success. Practices of Grit, Intellectual Humility and Curation are a much-needed code to live by in the legal profession. This book articulates ideas to build them, implement them and even track them through the new framework of the Personal Journey Map. *Leapfrog* is highly relatable, entertaining and a powerful read for every lawyer or professional who cares about their career'.

—**Karan Singh, Founding Partner, Trilegal**

LEAP FROG

SIX PRACTICES TO **THRIVE**

MUKESH SUD
PRIYANK NARAYAN

PENGUIN

VIKING

An imprint of Penguin Random House

VIKING

USA | Canada | UK | Ireland | Australia
New Zealand | India | South Africa | China

Viking is part of the Penguin Random House group of companies
whose addresses can be found at global.penguinrandomhouse.com

Published by Penguin Random House India Pvt. Ltd
4th Floor, Capital Tower 1, MG Road,
Gurugram 122 002, Haryana, India

First published in Viking by Penguin Random House India 2022
This revised edition published in 2023

10 9 8 7 6 5 4

ISBN 9780670096718

Typeset in Adobe Garamond Pro by Manipal Technologies Limited, Manipal
Printed at Thomson Press India Ltd, New Delhi

www.penguin.co.in

For our students,
who teach us
everyday

CONTENTS

INTRODUCTION

'A banana republic'.

This was O. Henry, the writer describing Honduras in 1904. The sobriquet has stuck.

This tropical country in Central America has another side. With more than 6,000 species of vascular plants, Honduras is known for its rainforests, hurricanes, and of course, bananas.

In 1996, the government wanted to build a bridge across the Choluteca River. Two years later, a Japanese firm completed construction of a 484-metre-long structure that spanned the river. A marvel of engineering, it was a proud moment for every Honduran. The locals christened it the 'Bridge of the Rising Sun'.

That year Honduras was hit by Hurricane Mitch. In four days, it brought six feet of rain, which the country normally got in six months. There was widespread destruction. Rivers flooded their banks and 7,000 people died. All the bridges in Honduras were damaged or destroyed, except one: the Choluteca Bridge.

There was, however, a problem. After the hurricane, the roads on either side of the bridge had disappeared. The river

had altered its course and now ran beside, not beneath, the bridge. The Choluteca Bridge became a bridge to nowhere.

The Choluteca Bridge is a metaphor for the uncertainty around us. It is a reminder that the problems we are attempting to solve may have changed.

Today, our mantra can no longer be 'built to last'. Rather it should be 'built to thrive'.

Leapfrog is a concept in industrial organizations where a new entrant moves ahead of its competitors. This is true for firms, societies, and even individuals. In each case, the incumbent, who is wedded to the status quo, fails to anticipate changes that a newer player can foresee. Economists tell us that leapfrogging is a response by smaller and more nimble players to significant changes in the external environment. During these times, prior experience and existing knowledge are worthless. They may even be a hindrance.

Like an agile firm you too can leapfrog to a new future. The research-based insights and curated stories in this book, will help you adopt a mindset and learn new practices to do that. These practices, and the pillars that support them, reinforce each other in ways you will soon discover.

We have taught at liberal education universities and business schools for nearly two decades. Many of the stories in this book are those of our students and alumni, who have taught us as much, and sometimes more, than we have taught them.

Using evidence-based outcomes and research across many disciplines, we have identified practices and pillars to help you thrive at work. We have woven stories and anecdotes around many of these concepts. This will enable you to connect the ideas in *Leapfrog* with your real-world experience.

We have drawn inferences from research and highlighted connections with the world of practice. We would like you to deliberate on these ideas and adopt those that work for you. We hope that the practices in this book, and the pillars that support them, will help you leapfrog to the future you want.

A Sneak Peek

The US Spelling Bee has been dubbed the 'Indian Superbowl'. Since 2008, 21 of the 24 champions have been of Indian origin. How did these Indian American children memorize so many words in the dictionary? They had grit. It helped them overcome obstacles and challenges to achieve their long-term goals. Recruiters at the United States Military Academy found that a grit score effectively identifies cadets who are likely to graduate than those who might quit. In Chapter 1 you will learn ways to develop grit by engaging in deliberate practice, refining your mental maps, and embracing boredom.

Do you realize that you are constantly being nudged when buying an airline ticket online, at the checkout counter while paying for groceries, and even when browsing a website? At Schiphol International Airport, the image of a small fly in a urinal nudges men to aim more accurately. This has reduced spillage by 80 per cent. Chapter 2 will show you how to nudge yourself. Making even incremental progress towards your goals and celebrating small wins could be one of them. By being aware of your biases, you can even nudge yourself to exercise regularly, play a musical instrument, or even join an online course.

Many of our students would like to work for Google. By learning to fail well, they can improve their chances of getting a job there. Companies want candidates with intellectual humility who accept limits to their knowledge and are ready to learn from others. Chapter 3 is about cultivating a growth mindset; writing a resume of your failures can be the first step in that journey.

Manjul Bhargava, one of the youngest tenured professors at Princeton, saw connections between maths, music, and Sanskrit. His ability to segue across disciplines has won him a Fields Medal, the equivalent of the Nobel Prize for mathematicians. In Chapter 4, you will learn about wicked problems and how dancing with disciplines will help you look at them differently. That is the reason teams with people from diverse backgrounds, from fiction writers and archaeologists to musicians and engineers, achieve better results. You will also find out the magic that can happen when ideas have sex.

How can you extract meaning and knowledge from the deluge of information around you? Find out in Chapter 5, which is about the art of curation. Using simple rules, curation will help you bring order to chaos and become better at making decisions. A study found that shoppers are 10 times more likely to buy jam when they have a choice of 6 flavours rather than 24. Those with fewer options were also happier with their purchase. To curate, you need to narrow your choices with simple rules and identify bullshit. That is why Warren Buffet wanted his personal pilot to have a 5/25 rule for his goals.

Do you remember the old proverb 'a bird in hand is worth two in the bush'? Well, it may be more relevant than you think. When the future is difficult to predict expert entrepreneurs depend on this, and other similar mantras to make decisions. In Chapter 6, you will also find out how the concept of a crazy quilt can help you create partnerships. Entrepreneurial thinking is more than just starting a venture; it can be an approach to life.

The practices in this book are building blocks you can use to navigate your future. The book concludes with a toolkit that will enable you to plan and work purposefully towards your goals. It will guide you through the steps to craft a *Personal Journey Map*. You will take stock of your current repertoire, identify the opportunities ahead and plan a way to get there. Many of our students have used the toolkit to imagine and then make a path towards their goals.

All the chapters in this book have a *So What?* section.

A student once asked:

> *Fine Professor,*
> *I have learnt a new practice and its underlying pillars.*
> *How can I use them?*

The *So What?* section will show you how.

The practices in *Leapfrog*, and their underlying pillars, will prevent your career getting disrupted, your education being outdated and your skills becoming irrelevant. Reading this book will ensure that, unlike the bridge over the Choluteca River, you will thrive.

Always.

Leapfrog: A Snapshot of 6 Practices and Pillars

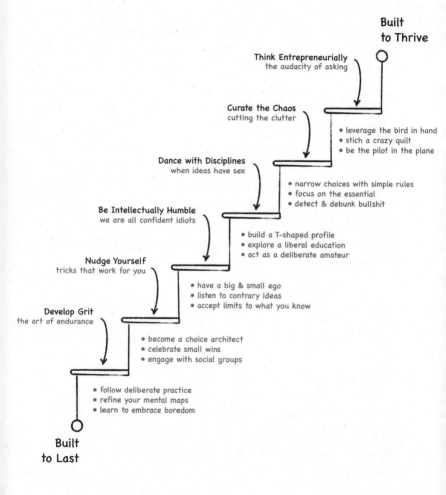

**Built
to Thrive**

Think Entrepreneurially
the audacity of asking

Curate the Chaos
cutting the clutter

- leverage the bird in hand
- stich a crazy quilt
- be the pilot in the plane

Dance with Disciplines
when ideas have sex

- narrow choices with simple rules
- focus on the essential
- detect & debunk bullshit

Be Intellectually Humble
we are all confident idiots

- build a T-shaped profile
- explore a liberal education
- act as a deliberate amateur

Nudge Yourself
tricks that work for you

- have a big & small ego
- listen to contrary ideas
- accept limits to what you know

Develop Grit
the art of endurance

- become a choice architect
- celebrate small wins
- engage with social groups

- follow deliberate practice
- refine your mental maps
- learn to embrace boredom

**Built
to Last**

1

DEVELOP GRIT

the art of endurance

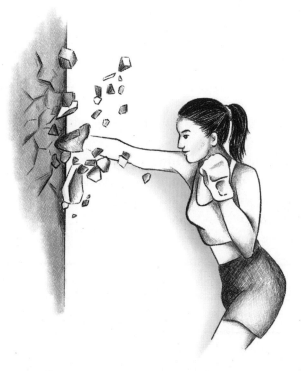

Are you familiar with these names?

Sameer Mishra (2008)	Kavya Shivashankar (2009)	Anamika Veeramani (2010)
Sukanya Roy (2011)	Snigdha Nandipati (2012)	Arvind Mahankali (2013)
Sriram Hathwar Ansun Sujoe (2014)	Vanya Shivashankar Gokul Venkataraman (2015)	Jairam Hathwar Nihar Janga (2016)
Ananya Vinay (2017)	Karthik Nemmamani (2018)	Rishik Gandhasri Erin Howard (2019)
Saketh Sundar Shruthika Padhy (2019)	Sohum Sukhatankar Abhijay Kodali (2019)	Christopher Serrao Rohan Raja (2019)

They are winners of the Scripps National Spelling Bee. Established in 1925 with nine participants, this contest has been held in the US every year, except during World War II and the Covid-19 pandemic. To take part, contestants must be under 15 and be studying in the eighth or a lower grade.

In 2019, 11 million children competed to be in the finals. The Spelling Bee's popularity rivals the New York Yankees and the Dallas Cowboys, two of America's most valuable sports franchises. Since 1994, the finals have been broadcast live, initially on ESPN and, more recently, on ION.

These are some of the words winners spelt in the finals.

guerdon	laodicean	stomuhr
cymotrichous	bougainvillea	knaidel
stichomythia	scherenschnitte	feldenkrais
marocoin	koinonia	guetapens

Don't worry if you haven't heard them, neither had we. Except for bougainvillea, and we needed help from a dictionary to spell it.

Did you notice anything unusual about the winners' names?

Most of them are of Indian origin. Indian Americans dominate the Spelling Bee, which has even been called the 'Indian Superbowl'.

In 2013, Arvind Mahankali won 30,000 dollars in cash and prizes for spelling 'knaidel'.* Interviewed on ESPN, Arvind maintained a Zen-like composure, as if the only worthy opponent left was spell check.

In the Netflix documentary *Spelling the Dream*, seven-year-old Akash Vukoti spells 'pneumonoultramicroscopicsilicovol canoconiosis'.†

The narrator says:

> *The only way the Indian American kids are losing the Spelling Bee [is] if they switch to Spanish next year and then it's still like 50:50.*

How do Indian American children like Arvind and Akash accomplish this?

The four-letter answer is GRIT.

To understand grit, we will travel to the world of Mozart, one of the most celebrated classical composers, and unravel his gifts. We will also find out why some cadets, after spending years preparing to join the United States Military Academy, quit before the programme even begins.

How can you develop grit?

---

* A dumpling eaten during Passover, the Jewish festival.
† A lung disease caused by inhaling fine ash and sand dust.

Grit rests on three pillars: follow deliberate practice, refine your mental maps, and learn to embrace boredom. You will find out from Steve Fallon, who, like most of us, could initially recall seven or eight digits of a number sequence read out to him. Wait to be surprised with his tally two years later. Finally, a 75-year longitudinal study at Harvard University unravelled a link between lifelong happiness and the grit to run on a treadmill at high speed for five minutes.

First, let us return to the 2019 Spelling Bee finals.

Jacques Bailly, a professor of Greek and Latin, was the official pronouncer. A former Spelling Bee winner, he would read a word aloud, explain its origin and give an example of its usage. The finalists had already spelt 47 words correctly in the last five rounds.

Jacques looked around at the eight of them:

> *We're throwing the dictionary at you and you're showing the dictionary whose boss. We are in uncharted territory.*

It was past midnight when the judges finally gave up. They had run out of words difficult enough to challenge the contestants. Meanwhile, the winners had coined a new word for themselves: *octochamps.*

Seven of the eight winners that year were Indian Americans. In 2022, Harini Logan of Texas was declared the winner. She beat 12-year-old Vikram Raju in a special speed round where each of them had to spell as many words as they could in 90 seconds. Vikram, a three-time participant, plans to return for a final attempt in 2023, hoping to become a Spelling Bee champion.

The 'Gift'

Travel back in time to the eighteenth century and the world of Leopold and his son Wolfgang Amadeus Mozart. Leopold's family wanted him to become a Catholic priest. He had other ambitions. Passionate about the theatre, Leopold began his career as a violinist and composer at the age of 21.

Despite being widely known, Leopold always felt that he had not received the acknowledgement he deserved. Keen to teach children music, he began with his family. At 11, Mozart's elder sister played the harpsichord and piano like a professional.

Watching his sister, Mozart began playing musical instruments and soon became the focus of his father's attention. In 1763, *The Augsburger Intelligenz-Zettel* carried an anonymous letter about the young Mozart:

> *I saw and heard how, when he was made to listen in another room, they would give him notes, now high, now low, not only on the pianoforte but on every other imaginable instrument as well, and he came out with the letter name of the note in an instant. Indeed, on hearing a bell toll or a clock, or even a pocket watch strike, he was able at the same moment to name the note of the bell or timepiece.*

Mozart was believed to be born with perfect or absolute pitch, the ability to identify a musical note without the benefit of a reference tone. Less than 1 in 10,000 musicians can recreate or differentiate notes without listening to an external reference.

At 5, Mozart was playing the violin and piano; at 8, he wrote his first symphony; and at 17, he had a job at the renowned Salzburg court. Fame followed Mozart as he displayed his talents across courts in Europe. By 21, he had composed Piano Concerto No. 9, an early masterpiece that captivated the aristocracy of that era.

Can we explain Mozart's precociousness and rise to fame on the twin gifts of perfect pitch and natural talent?

There is a twist in this tale.

Anders Ericsson, a Swedish psychologist and academic, spent a lifetime studying expertise and human performance. He wanted to answer a simple question: How do some people become world-class in fields like chess, medicine, music, or sports. Ericsson discovered a more nuanced view about Mozart's dual gifts.

Chinese Tones

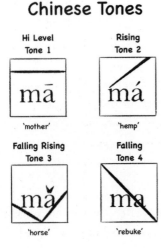

First, let's understand Mozart's perfect pitch. We now know that many children who speak Norwegian, Mandarin and Punjabi have perfect pitch. In these languages, similar words have different meanings depending on the tone and emphasis with which they are spoken.

For example, in Mandarin, the syllable 'ma' can be spoken in four tones. When the vowel is pronounced in a high-level tone, it means 'mother'. It means 'hemp'* in a rising tone; 'horse' when spoken in a falling and then rising tone; and is a rebuke when used in a falling tone. While first learning their mother tongue, infants quickly pick up these variations in tone.

A study examined children between the ages of two and six who were enrolled in a music school in Tokyo. The children were trained at home on their piano for between two and five minutes a day. Initially, none of them had perfect pitch. About a year later, 88 per cent had acquired perfect pitch. The remaining students had stopped training for reasons unconnected with the study. We now know that until they are about six, children can be trained to acquire perfect pitch.

Let's now examine Mozart's other gift: his natural talent. Mozart had, at a young age, performed in many cities across Europe, including Vienna, Munich, Prague, and Paris. Travelling across Europe, Mozart was exposed to a variety of local music traditions. In London, he met the German composer Johann Christian Bach. Well-known in that era, Bach held an early sway over Mozart and even influenced his concerto style.

As a child, Mozart was under the guidance of his father. Leopold's treatise on playing the violin was published the year Mozart was born. The book was later translated into Dutch and French and had two German editions. Leopold had earlier tested many of his pedagogical ideas on Mozart's elder sister who went on to become an accomplished musician.

Are maestros born or made? Do sportspersons achieve perfection with their natural ability or through hard work? To

---

* A plant used to make rope.

what extent can you improve your memory with deliberate practice?

These are some of the questions we will explore in the rest of this chapter.

Violinists at the Berlin Academy of Music were divided into three groups. The first group had the potential to become world-class performers. The second were considered good, while violinists in the third group were expected to become music teachers. Ericsson and his colleagues discovered that violinists in all three groups had very similar musical biographies. They had all been taught by comparable music teachers, been exposed to similar musical instruments, and had been practising since they were about six years old.

The difference between the three groups was the total hours they had been practising music since childhood. The prospective music teachers averaged 4,000 hours, good violinists 8,000 and potential world-class performers over 10,000 hours. Ericsson also studied pianists and reached the same conclusion.

Ten thousand hours is the equivalent of practising four hours a day for seven years. How do some people train for such long periods to achieve their goal?

As we saw earlier with the Indian American Spelling Bee competitors, one factor is grit, which is the ability to pursue your goals with passion and perseverance. That ultimately leads to perfection.

Perseverance and Perfection

Angela Duckworth is a psychologist and professor at the University of Pennsylvania. She is a recipient of a MacArthur

Fellowship—also known as a genius grant—for her work in understanding the role of grit in educational and professional achievement.

As a PhD student, Duckworth wondered why some people succeed in achieving their long-term goals, while others give up. Looking for a context where people may be quitting too early, she studied cadets training to become officers at the United States Military Academy at West Point.[*]

Selection to West Point is competitive, rivalling elite universities like Harvard and Stanford. Besides being at the top of their class in school, candidates must demonstrate leadership qualities and be in excellent physical condition. Applicants also need a letter of recommendation from their Senator or member of Congress. Some have even managed to get a recommendation from the Vice President of United States.

Candidates begin preparing for West Point many years in advance. In their junior year of high school, about 12,000 students start the application process, 4,000 get a nomination, and 2,500 manage to clear the cut-off required by the army. Of this number, 1,200 are finally selected. West Point graduates are often referred to as 'The Long Grey Line' for the colour of their uniforms and the prestige they command. Graduating from West Point has been described as 'making history and chasing greatness'.

Surprisingly, after years of planning and preparation, many candidates drop out. Some leave even before training begins. To mark the transition from civilian to military life, cadets attend an initiation programme nicknamed 'Beast Barracks'. Over a

---

[*] The United States Military Academy is popularly known as West Point for its location north of New York overlooking the Hudson River.

period of 6 weeks, they deal with numerous physical and mental challenges, often toiling for 17 hours a day in classrooms and on the field.

After aspiring for years to become military officers Duckworth wondered why some candidates quit the programme so early. Realizing that about 15 per cent of the cadets fail to graduate, recruiters had begun to question their selection criteria. Over the years they had tried several methods. Initially, they had used a 'Whole Candidate Score' that accounted for a cadet's school ranking, leadership ability, physical fitness, and scores on standardized tests. Despite years of testing, recruiters found that this score did not reliably predict the likelihood that a cadet would make it through 'Beast Barracks'. Attempts to predict performance using intelligence tests too had limited validity. In another method of evaluation, candidates were shown picture postcards and asked to imagine stories from them. It was hoped that those who described brave and courageous acts would have a better chance of graduating.

Duckworth and her colleagues made the cadets at West Point answer a questionnaire. The questions had no connection to talent or intelligence or even the 'Whole Candidate Score' used earlier. Instead, it measured a cadet's passion and perseverance—their ability to stay motivated when confronted with unfavourable circumstances. Duckworth called it grit.

Compared to earlier tests, grit better predicted whether a cadet would drop out or complete 'Beast Barracks'. Since then, independent studies have corroborated many of those initial findings. Sales employees with grit are more likely to keep their jobs, individuals with grit tend to remain married, and students with grit are more likely to graduate from high school. At an

Ivy League university, undergraduates who scored higher on grit earned better GPAs than their peers despite having lower SAT scores.

Besides grit, there are other ways to predict whether individuals will persevere in adverse or stressful circumstances to achieve their goals. We have focussed on grit for two reasons.

First, grit has an intuitive appeal and is easy to understand. For example, those enrolled in online courses realize that grittier learners are more likely to complete the programme. We know that from chess players to contestants in the Spelling Bee, from musicians to military officers, people with grit perform better and are more likely to achieve their long-term goals.

Second, grit can be measured. As educators, we are excited that our students can, by answering a questionnaire, find out and then improve on their grit scores. As Peter Drucker said:

You can't improve what you don't measure.

Irrespective of your grit score, you can develop and even make grit a habit by recognizing its underlying pillars.

A widely used grit scale has 10 questions. Read each question and select the box that is your best response. Your score is the sum of the points in the boxes divided by 10.

The highest score is 5; the lowest is 1. As a reference, a grit score of 4.3 would put you in the top 20 per cent of those who have taken the test. Remember the score reflects how you perceive yourself; others may view you differently. Over time as you try and develop grit, your score will also improve.

S.No	Self-Statement	Not at all like me	Not much like me	Some-what like me	Mostly like me	Very much like me
1	I sometimes get distracted from existing projects by new ideas	5	4	3	2	1
2	I am not discouraged by setbacks and don't give up easily	1	2	3	4	5
3	I often set a goal but later choose to pursue a different one	5	4	3	2	1
4	I am a hard worker	1	2	3	4	5
5	I have difficulty in maintaining my focus on projects that take more than a few months to complete	5	4	3	2	1
6	I finish whatever I begin	1	2	3	4	5
7	My interests change from year to year	5	4	3	2	1
8	I am diligent and never give up	1	2	3	4	5
9	I have been obsessed with a certain idea or project for a short time but later lost interest in it	5	4	3	2	1
10	I have overcome setbacks to conquer an important challenge	1	2	3	4	5

Understanding Grit

From existing research and our own teaching experience, we have identified three pillars that support grit. First, you must learn to practise deliberately. This is different from normal or regular practice, with which you are probably familiar. Second, over a period, you need to refine the mental maps or images of the activity you are engaged with. Finally, rather than fight boredom, you must learn to accept and even embrace the monotony of doing a task repeatedly.

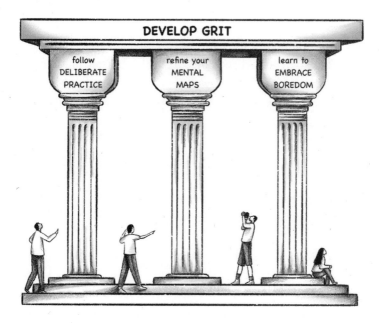

Follow Deliberate Practice

In *Outliers: The Story of Success*, Malcolm Gladwell popularized the 10,000-hour rule. To become world-class in any field, he suggested you need to just practise 20 hours a week for 10 years.

An often-quoted story is that of Shizuka Arakawa, the Japanese figure skater who won a gold medal at the 2006 Winter Olympics. One of her moves in the skating rink involved jumping and bending backwards with her feet pointed in opposite directions. Shizuka began skating when she was five. Over the next 19 years, she probably fell on the ice about 20,000 times, while cushioned only by a thin costume.

Perfection and excellence, however, require more than practice over many years. This is one of the myths surrounding practice. While performing the same task repeatedly may help you clock 10,000 hours, it is only with deliberate practice that you can become an expert and achieve perfection.

The difference between practice and deliberate practice can be understood with the power of an exponent. Suppose you practise 365 days a year. With regular practice, you repeat the same task every day.

With deliberate practice, rather than mindless repetition, you ensure that every attempt is one per cent better than your previous effort. Practicing deliberately will make you 37 times better at any task than you were at the beginning of the year.

$$(1.00)^{365} - 1.00$$
$$(1.01)^{365} - 37.7$$

Ericsson, the researcher whose work on human performance we read about earlier, experimented with an undergraduate student Steve Fallon (referred to as SF in academic literature). He wanted to find out the extent to which SF's memory could improve with deliberate practice. Ericsson would read out numbers to SF at the rate of one per second. After a pause of 20 seconds, SF would try to recall the series. Training began with a random five-digit sequence.

This sequence of 22 numbers was later read out to SF:

4131778406034948709462

In *Talent Is Overrated*, Geoff Colvin narrates how SF recalled these numbers:

> *All right, all right, all right, he muttered, as Ericsson, the researcher in the study, read out the list to him.*

*All right! All right. Oh . . . geez! He clapped his hands
loudly three times, then grew quiet and seemed to
focus further.*
Okay. Okay . . . four, thirteen point one, he yelled.
He was breathing heavily.
Seventy-seven, eighty-four.
He was nearly screaming.
Oh, six oh three.
Now he was screaming.
Forty-nine, four, eighty-seven, oh.
Pause.
Ninety-four, six.
Screeching now. Only one digit left. But it isn't there.
*Ninety-four, six point . . . oh, ninety-four, six
point . . .*
He was screaming and sounding desperate.
Finally, hoarse and strangled.
TWO.

As Ericsson checked and confirmed the results, there was a
knock on the door. It was the campus police responding to a
call of someone screaming in the lab.

After two years of deliberate practice, SF could recall
82 digits.

Let's understand the elements of deliberate practice. It
involves becoming an expert in any field by:

- receiving feedback from a coach and working on it,
- gradually moving out of your comfort zone, and
- doing things you are not good at.

Practice	Deliberate Practice
• Thoughtless repetition	• Improvement with every repetition
• Doing things you are good at	• Moving beyond your comfort zone
• Watching an expert perform	• Having an expert mentor
• Training and giving feedback to others	• Receiving constructive feedback

Renowned violinist Nathan Milstein was said to be concerned about the long hours those around him were practising. He approached his mentor on how long he should practise. This was the answer he got:

If you practise with your fingers, no amount is enough.
If you practise with your head, two hours is plenty.

While this may have been said partly in jest, practising for long hours is not enough to become an expert. We will use SF's ability to recall numbers to explain the first two elements of deliberate practice. For the third, we will venture into ice skating.

Deliberate practice requires the presence of a coach who can provide detailed feedback. SF knew how he had performed, both when he had done well on a number sequence and when he was wrong. SF internalized Ericsson's feedback, paying particular attention to aspects that were causing him a problem. The two would then work on SF's technique, often improving it or even developing a new one. As the study progressed, SF became proficient at identifying numbers that posed a challenge and found ways to work around it.

Second, Ericsson initially set SF goals that were within his capability before gradually increasing them. When SF got the correct answer, Ericsson added one number to the string. If he faltered, Ericsson reduced the length of the string by two and repeated the exercise. SF was always in a space where the challenge was only slightly greater than his capability at that time.

For the third element of deliberate practice, let us return to Shizuka, the skater who is estimated to have fallen 20,000 times on ice. A year before the 2006 Olympics, she was placed ninth at the World Championship. Shizuka had been struggling with her motivation and even mulled retirement.

Unwilling to leave the skating rink on a low note, Shizuka decided to make one last attempt to regain the top spot. She needed a method to take her performance to the next level.

Over the course of her career Shizuka had worked with eight coaches. Just two months before the 2006 Olympics, Shizuka signed up with yet another coach. It was Nikolai Morozov, a former Olympic ice dancer from Belarus who had previously been her choreographer. Nikolai changed Shizuka's music and routine. This is unusual in figure skating, where a dancer's programme is perfected to the minutest detail over many years of practice.

Working with a different technique, Shizuka became the first Japanese skater to win a gold medal at an Olympic event. In a sport dominated by teenagers, she was the oldest female champion in eight decades. After retiring from competitive skating, Shizuka was elected to the World Figure Skating Hall of Fame.

Shizuka is an elite skater. Elite skaters differ from sub-elites who do well but don't make it to the top level. Sub-elites concentrate on perfecting tasks that they are already good at. In contrast, elite skaters spend a higher proportion of their time on what they are not doing well. They also focus on those jumps and combinations they need to excel at in order to win medals.

Will your performance keep improving if you practise deliberately?

Over many repetitions, even the performance of experts will gradually plateau. When the performance curve flattens, the mental maps or images experts have developed over time need to be refined or even changed.

Refine Your Mental Maps

Our brains have an in-built navigational system which formulates a mental map of any task we are doing. These maps can also be called mental models or images.

Imagine driving home one evening while listening to music and thinking about dinner. You are aware of the condition of the road, the other vehicles around and even the two-wheeler trying to overtake you. Intuitively, you have a feel for the accelerator and brake and know when to change gears. Over time and many repetitions, you construct a mental map that you automatically follow.

Now, imagine driving a rental car in a different country. You are on the opposite side of the road and perhaps driving an automatic transmission you are not familiar with. You need to revise your mental map. This new one will gradually get embedded in your long-term memory. Over time, you will be as comfortable in this setting as while driving at home. This is how mental maps are redrawn or refined.

While working with SF, Ericsson realized that short-term memory, with its ability to hold six to eight numbers, would not be enough. Our long-term memory does not have the same limitation. We remember our birthdays (and hopefully our spouses' too), important phone numbers, and email passwords. These are examples of retrieving information, which, through repetition, gets embedded in our long-term memory.

Ericsson and SF formulated mental maps around running times. SF was a long-distance runner who followed world events and races. He began to connect numbers with running times he was familiar with. For example, 907 was a good time for a 2-mile run when thought of as 9 minutes and 7 seconds. With this, 907 was no longer a random number but one that SF could recall from his long-term memory. SF would break a sequence of numbers into four- or five-digit sets, followed by a six-digit group at the end. He would repeat the last group to himself several times until he remembered it by its sound.

As with driving, we have mental images of everything we do. However, the quality of the images and how frequently we use and can retrieve them depends on our expertise. Experts develop complex mental images that they can control precisely. This helps them improve their performance. Experts also constantly refine their mental maps and recall them quickly.

Expert chess players often play multiple boards while blindfolded. They do not depend on their memory of where pieces are placed. In a randomly placed chessboard, the memory of experts, intermediate players, and beginners is very similar. Expert chess players, however, recognize patterns of attack and defence and create mental images around them. They then store these images in their long-term memory and recall them at will.

We all have a natural tendency to see patterns and make connections. It helps us compress data, and then store and recall it when required. This is also called chunking, where experts group pieces of information into meaningful chunks based on patterns that they are familiar with.

Michael Phelps, one of the most decorated swimmers, has won 28 Olympic medals. At the Beijing Olympics in 2008, Phelps climbed onto the starting block for the 200-metre butterfly event. As the world-record holder, he was expected to dominate the race.

Diving into the water, Phelps realized he was in trouble. That day he had worn two swimming caps to hold his goggles in place. Despite this, water began seeping through them. It got worse as the race progressed. When Phelps was on the last lap, his goggles were filled with water:

> *I could not see the line at the bottom of the pool. I could not see the black T marks that convey the wall. I could not see anybody else in other lanes. I could not see.*

Phelps and his coach Bob Bowman had planned for this eventuality. Bowman was known to crush Phelps's goggles under his feet and made him swim without them. Before an event, he would make Phelps close his eyes and imagine a mental map of the race. At the end of each practice, Bowman would tell Phelps to watch the *videotape* before going to sleep and then once again the following morning. The videotape Bowman was referring to was not a tape at all, just a mental representation of a perfect race.

Lying in bed, Phelps would picture the initial dive off the starting block, his strokes, the flip against the wall, and finally, the glide at the end. Over many years of refining his mental maps, he knew the number of strokes, the intuitive feel of the perfect stroke, and if he was deviating from it. That day in Beijing, Phelps won the gold medal and set a new world record.

Imagine deliberately practising a task for many years while creating and refining your mental maps. Most of us would get bored.

Wouldn't you?

Learn to Embrace Boredom

It is the first day of a new term. As students shuffle into class, they glance around for a friend or a familiar face. Some remain glued to their phones.

Recently, a student told us about Holly Thompson, a British teenager. During a politics class, Holly felt bored and yawned. No damage so far, except perhaps to the professor's fragile ego. Unfortunately, Holly's yawn was so wide that she dislocated her jaw and could not shut her mouth. A friend tried to help but only caused Holly more pain. The school nurse even tried using ice packs on the jaw, without success.

Finally, Holly had to be taken to the local hospital where doctors freed her jaw. After narrating this story, the student wanted permission to use her device in class. She didn't want to dislocate her jaw as Holly did.

Boredom is a challenge even in sports. We tend to believe that elite sportspersons are privileged and must enjoy what they do. However, even professional, amateur, and college athletes are often bored.

In *Atomic Habits*, James Clear suggests that to stay focussed, you need to *fall in love with boredom*. To many, this may sound like an oxymoron. One way around is to break the end goal into smaller sub-goals and monitor your progress. We have built on this idea with the progress principle and celebrating small wins in the next chapter.

Let's return to the Spelling Bee contestants and find out how they spent years with the dictionary mastering words with Greek, French, and Latin roots.

While practising, participants used three strategies to memorize spellings. As a leisure activity, participants read for pleasure and played word games where spellings were incidental. Second, they would get their family members and friends to quiz them. Some took help of a mobile app or a computer programme. Their third strategy involved the solitary practice of word spellings as well as their root words and history.

Which strategy do you think would be the most effective? Which is likely to be the most boring?

The third.

This is also true for musicians and chess players. The Spelling Bee participants, however, devised a way to make practice fun and playful. One contestant would spell words into a microphone that was connected to an electric piano and recorded her voice. Playing back the words she had just spelt made her practice playful.

Another participant would take frequent breaks during her preparation and play the guitar for a while. One made her grandmother the word pronouncer. Grandma's phonetic pronunciation of words was often hilarious. This would lead to much laughter all around.

The children began to enjoy the feeling of becoming an expert at spellings. This relieved their boredom. Uma, one of the contestants, felt that once you start something, you cannot quit halfway. Over time, the results gave her a feeling of joy:

> *When you mastered it, it's like, 'Yay, ask me spelling',*
> *cuz you got them all right.*

Years after the event, contestants were asked what they had enjoyed the most. Many remembered the fun they had in their study groups at the hotel and while competing in the finals.

The path to your long-term goals will be challenging and will include dealing with boredom. You must find ways to alleviate it by making the activity fun and playful. Results too can become a source of joy and add pleasure to your work.

So What?

> *You might have more talent than me, you might*
> *be smarter than me, you might be sexier than me,*
> *you might be all of these things—you got me in nine*
> *categories. But if we get on a treadmill together,*

*there's two things: You're getting off first or I am
going to die. It's really that simple.*
                              —Will Smith (American actor)

Can a poor kid from Philadelphia win five Golden Globe
nominations, two Academy Awards, and four Grammys by
being able to run on a treadmill? A Harvard University study on
psychological health might tell us more.

It was 1938. Sophomore students at Harvard University
were asked to run on a treadmill for five minutes. The students
were unaware that the settings on the treadmill were so steep and
fast that it was virtually impossible to complete the challenge.
Researchers wanted to find out the extent to which students
were willing to push themselves. They wondered at what point
would they step off the machine?

The study began with 268 men.* Many students dropped
out of the challenge, some as early as a minute and a half after
starting. The average time on the treadmill was four minutes,
with only a few managing to stay on it for the entire five.
Originally called the Grant Study, this was later expanded with
new cohorts and included the wives of the participants. It is now
known as the Harvard Study of Adult Development.

The participants were interviewed every two years. They
were asked about their careers, social activities, work, and
marriage. They disclosed details about their bank balances,
how happy they were, number of visits to a psychiatrist, their
career advancement, and even whether they used drugs or
tranquilisers. Data collected over seven decades has made this

---

* Harvard University did not admit women at that time.

one of the longest and most comprehensive surveys on ageing and happiness.

Time spent on the treadmill was found to be a reliable predictor of psychological well-being. Those who managed five minutes on the treadmill earned more, had happier marriages and lower rates of depression. Endurance on the treadmill also correlated better with successful relationships than it did even with health.

For the 1938 cohort of Harvard University, it wasn't intelligence that mattered. Not even talent. It was their ability to persevere and develop grit that revealed how happy and successful they would be later in life.

2

NUDGE YOURSELF

tricks that work for you

Professor: Why do men sprinkle when they tinkle?
A few smiles, some uneasy glances.
Professor: You are a manager of an airport terminal. The cleaning crew complains of puddles on the floor in the men's toilet. What would you do?
An awkward silence.
(An image pops up on a screen in the classroom)

There is laughter in the class.
Professor: What else can you do?
The class is silent.
Professor: Will this help?
(Another image pops up on the screen)

Aad Kieboom, a manager at Schiphol International Airport in Amsterdam, etched an image of a fly inside a urinal. Spillage reduced by 80 per cent. Men, it appears, like aiming, especially when they think they can wash things away. As researchers, we can't help wondering, how the spillage was measured.

This chapter is about nudging to change the behaviour of individuals and groups. In the corporate world, McKinsey & Company found that nudging their managers made them more creative. Virgin Atlantic airlines saved nearly 7,000 tonnes of fuel by nudging pilots to be carbon neutral and fuel efficient. The world's largest behavioural nudge has been taking place across villages and towns in India.

You will also find out about default options and how they have increased rates of organ donation in Europe. Would you like to nudge yourself to achieve an objective? For that, learn to be a choice architect, celebrate small wins, and engage with your social groups.

Do you know that students who set their own deadlines on assignments do better than those who have no deadline at all?

There is a dark side to nudging too. Scott Stevens had a gambling problem and secretly spent his savings playing on slot machines at his favourite casino. Scott's story has a lesson for all of us.

Finally, you will find out how four of our students nudged themselves to achieve their goals.

Understanding a Nudge

Nudging helps people make better choices without limiting the options available to them.

Richard Thaler, winner of the 2017 Nobel Prize for his work in behavioural economics, popularized nudging as a way to influence behaviour without restricting choices. Nudges differ from mandates. In a cafeteria, banning fast food is a mandate; placing vegetables and fruits at eye level to encourage their consumption is a nudge.

Objectives can be achieved by a mandate or with a gentle nudge. Which do you think will work better?

Objective	Mandate	Nudge
Get children to tidy their room	Instruct children: 'clean your room'	Play 'tidy my room' game with children
Use stairs rather than escalators	Disable escalators	Mark stairs with calories used while climbing
Healthy eating habits	Limit servings	Provide smaller plates, keep healthy food in front
Control energy consumption	Allot fixed units per household	Keep households aware of neighbours' consumption

Another way of nudging people is to add an element of fun or playfulness to what they are doing. Volkswagen, the German automobile company, wanted people to embrace a healthier lifestyle. They decided to nudge commuters at a metro station to climb stairs rather than use the escalator. Stairs at a Stockholm metro station were made to look like the keyboard of a piano. When people walked on them, each step emitted a musical note. With this, the number of people using the stairs increased by

66 per cent. Many commuters even ran up and down for fun. Piano staircases have now sprung up in other cities.

Ask a football fan who is a bigger icon: Cristiano Ronaldo or Lionel Messi? A transparent bin outside a London tube station lets passers-by vote with their cigarette butts.

Do you want to keep your neighbourhood clean?

Try turning a garbage bin into a voting machine with a choice between:

- Shah Rukh vs Salman
- Federer vs Nadal
- Bradman vs Tendulkar

All these examples involve an element of fun. Purists might argue that adding an incentive disqualifies it from being a nudge.

We leave it to you to decide.

Nudging a Community

Maya Shankar, a cognitive scientist, is the Global Director of Behavioural Science at Google. As an advisor to the Obama administration, she noticed that very few veterans were signing up for government-funded educational and job assistance programmes.

Maya decided to nudge them:

> *Instead of telling veterans that they were eligible for the program, we simply reminded them that they had earned it through their years of service.*

Replacing the word *eligible* with *earned* increased the number of veterans accessing the programme by 9 per cent.

In the 1980s, a nudge campaign was launched in Texas. At that time, people dumped garbage on the roads and even threw it out of moving vehicles. Every year, the state spent 20 million dollars on clearing litter. A survey found that men between the ages of 18 and 35 were the most likely to litter.

The Department of Transportation began a campaign to discourage littering. Their slogan, 'Don't Mess with Texas', became popular across the country. It was on the radio, on merchandise in gift shops and on billboards across highways. People even had it as bumper stickers on their cars.

In television commercials, members of the Dallas Cowboys collected empty beer cans from the road, crushed them in their hands and threatened: 'Don't mess with Texas'. In the first six years of the campaign, roadside litter on highways reduced by 72 per cent.

* * *

India is using behavioural nudges to address a sanitation crisis. In 2014, about 550 million people defecated in fields or on roadsides. The government launched the Swachh Bharat Mission (SBM) to build toilets and get people to use them. Earlier attempts had focussed primarily on providing toilets with little emphasis on changing behaviour.

Parameswaran (Param) Iyer is an Indian Civil Servant and the CEO of NITI Aayog.* He specializes in sanitation and water. Watching television one day, Param nearly fell off his chair. It was 15 August 2014, and the Indian Prime Minister was speaking of open defecation and the indignity women faced. This subject was taboo in India and never discussed in polite society.

Param returned to India to head the SBM initiative. Given the nation's diversity, the number of languages and dialects spoken, and vast cultural differences, the team wondered how nudging would work. The fight against open defecation would have to be a *jan andolan,* a people's movement.

Worldwide nudge campaigns have succeeded when they:

- are *easy* to understand,
- are *attractive* in their messaging,
- use the power of *social* relationships, and
- are *timely*.

Easy	Attractive
• Harness the strength of defaults • Reduce the hassle in taking up the service • Simplify messages	• Catch attention • Design rewards and sanctions for maximum impact
Social	**Timely**
• Show that most people perform the desired behaviour • Use the power of networks • Encourage people to commit and get others to commit	• Prompt people when they are the most receptive • Consider immediate costs and benefits • Help people plan their response to events

---

* National Institute for Transforming India, Government of India.

This framework, known by its acronym EAST, has been widely adopted to implement behavioural change. Let's see how SBM operationalized some aspects of this framework in the field.

Trendsetters were made change agents and encouraged to get others to spread the message to nearby villages. They were instructed to generate a feeling of disgust towards open defecation. Using the example of houseflies, and underground water sources, communities were made to realize that they were effectively eating each other's waste. In villages and towns, agents were told to use the crudest word for defecation—essentially the local language equivalent of *shit*—in their messaging.

Volunteers gathered at popular defecation spots. They would greet open defecators with a namaste, a polite smile and flowers. Village panchayats were given ownership of the mission. Those aligned with SBM's vision used social pressure on non-conformers within their own communities.

Movie stars Amitabh Bachchan and Anushka Sharma were made SBM's brand ambassadors. *Toilet: Ek Prem Katha*, a Bollywood movie, became popular. It was the story of a young

bride who had access to a toilet in her parents' home. After marriage she was expected to join a 'lota party'* at her in-laws' place. Unable to persuade her husband to construct a toilet at home, she files

---

* A colloquial term for a group of people heading to the fields to defecate, each carrying a mug of water (*lota*).

for divorce. The satirical comedy ends with the government agreeing to construct toilets for the entire village. The movie reinforced and spread a message that communities should shun open defecation.

Param's approach has paid dividends:

> *Swachh Bharat Mission has, perhaps, at a scale unimaginable to Thaler (the Noble prize winner), nudged rural communities in India to change their habit of open defecation.*

Default Options

After completing a mid-career PhD in India, Mukesh (author), moved to the US. This is his story.

In the fall of 2006, I joined a university in Illinois. A month later, HR (human resources) sent me an email:

> *Professor, on your pension plan, please select a portfolio from the options available. We will invest your, and the university's contribution, in that account.*

Options included bonds and money markets, target dated funds and various combination of stocks. The email detailed past trends and future projections. A few weeks later, HR sent a reminder. This was followed by a call that went into voicemail.

Between teaching for the first time and adjusting to life in a new country, the messages were unanswered. The first term ended. Colleagues and students had begun to like the 'foreigner with a funny accent'. After grading the end-term exam, I got back to HR with an investment portfolio.

At the end of the year, I realized that the university had contributed to my plan for only six months. Their contribution started from the date I selected a portfolio and not my date of joining. The university's contribution for six months was lost. It was three times my share. For a 'fresh off the boat' immigrant, the loss of 5,000 dollars rankled.

Suppose the initial email from HR had added:

> *Most of our faculty opt for 'plan X'. Unless we hear to the contrary, we will invest in it. You can change this at any time at no additional cost.*

This is an example of a default option. It requires you to opt out, rather than opt in. You are automatically included unless you decide otherwise.

Using a default option has increased organ donation rates in many countries. European nations generally follow either *explicit* consent, where you must opt in to be a donor, or *presumed* consent, where you are assumed to be a donor unless you opt out.

Germany has an opt-in policy, while Austria follows an opt-out one. The two neighbours are culturally alike, yet Germany's consent rate is 12 per cent, whereas Austria's is 99 per cent. This trend is prevalent across European countries that follow either of the two policies.

Are default options always good for you?

You need to be careful. Consider a subscription to a magazine or a journal. Many of them will automatically renew your subscription unless you opt out. The next time you buy an airline ticket, notice if you are automatically charged a rupee towards reducing carbon emissions or given the option to add it to the cost of the ticket.

Priyank (author) was enjoying the breakfast buffet at a hotel in Singapore. He noticed a message on his table mat: 'We weigh leftovers in your plate and charge two dollars per kg for wasted food'. In fine print: 'Charges will be billed to your room'.

Another way to nudge people is by telling them what others do. Suppose your hotel room carried this sign: 'Nine out of ten guests who stayed in this room reused their towel'.

Seeing this sign, would you be more likely to hang your towel on a rack or throw it into the laundry bag?

Nudging has succeeded in promoting social objectives. Let's see how effective it can be at work.

Nudges at the Workplace

Can a cup of hot tea or coffee increase your creativity?

At a McKinsey & Company leadership programme in Australia, senior executives were divided into two groups. Working in pairs, participants were asked for suggestions to improve an upcoming leadership programme. One group, who received a folder with the message 'Hello! we need your help', were served cups of hot tea or coffee. Executives in the second group were offered cold  water and given a bureaucratic memo: 'Please adhere to these instructions'.

Participants in the first group had 70 new ideas; those in the second group made 32 suggestions, many of which were mundane. McKinsey & Company concluded that even seasoned professionals can benefit from subtle interventions, and small stimuli can result in appreciable outcomes. The company now has a database of over 80 nudges and 150 interventions that are customizable to drive desired behaviours.

Do you know about the observer effect?

Simply put, it means that people change their behaviour when they know they are being watched.

At a garment factory, researchers were examining the effect of working conditions on output. The workers at the factory were aware of the study and knew they were being observed.

When lighting on the shop floor was improved, productivity increased. The conditions were then gradually reversed to see if productivity would go back to previous levels. Output, however, continued to rise, until workers were practically stitching in the dark. Realizing that they were being observed, workers had changed their behaviour. This is also called the Hawthorne Effect, after the factory in Illinois where the original study took place.

* * *

Virgin Atlantic airlines wanted to be carbon neutral and make their pilots fuel efficient. Over an eight-month period, the airline studied fuel consumption during three phases of flying: pre-flight (take-off), in-flight (mid-air), and post-flight (taxiing). Fuel consumption in each phase depends on decisions that pilots take on speed, altitude, and route. During landing, for example, pilots decide when engines should be shut down while the aircraft is taxiing to its parking slot.

Pilots were randomly assigned to four groups. Amongst pilots in the control group,* it was business as usual. As in the past, they continued to get standard fuel-efficiency feedback. The three

---

* In an experiment, a control group is one in which nothing is changed.

experimental groups were, however, given targets, some of which were linked to incentives. They also received pointers on their performance and were encouraged to work towards their goals.

The study found:

> *Notifying captains [pilots] that fuel efficiency is being studied, as well as providing them with tailored information, targets, and feedback, are cost-effective methods for changing behaviours and achieving fuel, carbon, and cost savings.*

Surprisingly, pilots in the control group also saved fuel. Just being told that they were part of a study nudged pilots in this group to be more environment friendly while flying their aircraft. As a result of this study, 7,000 tonnes of fuel were saved and 22,000 tonnes of carbon dioxide emissions were avoided.

We have seen examples of nudging people to achieve social and professional goals. Let's find out how you can nudge yourself to reach your personal goals.

Beating Your Biases

Odysseus, the legendary Greek King of Ithaca, was sailing home after having won the Trojan War. Goddess Circe had warned him about the Sirens, the beautiful enchantresses whose irresistible singing lured sailors to their death on the rocky shores of their island. Recognizing his vulnerability, Odysseus made his crew tie him to the ship's mast. They were instructed not to set him free under any circumstances. Meanwhile the crew's ears were plugged with beeswax to ensure they were not beguiled by the Sirens.

Hearing the Sirens sing, Odysseus begged to be untied. Following orders, the crew ignored his pleas and sailed on. According to the tale, the Sirens were fated to die if someone heard them sing and escaped unharmed. After the ship sailed past, the Sirens threw themselves in the sea and perished.

Odysseus had created an environment that prevented him from falling prey to the Sirens. This is known as a 'commitment device'. Students often resort to it when they realize that they will benefit by committing themselves to a course of action.

According to Dan Ariely, a professor of psychology and behavioural economics at Duke University, decisions on the food we eat, the car we drive, and even the life partner we choose are often not made judiciously. We tend to be irrational. Fortunately, we are all *predictably irrational*.

Knowing your weakness, can you nudge yourself to make better decisions?

Three pillars will help you to nudge yourself. First, set up the right choice architecture, that is, the environment in which you will be taking a decision. Second, celebrate small wins to generate momentum to reach your goals. Finally, engage with your social groups.

NUDGE YOURSELF

| become a CHOICE ARCHITECT | celebrate SMALL WINS | engage with SOCIAL GROUPS |

Become a Choice Architect

Choice architecture is the way choices are presented. It influences how you think about choices and can affect your decision. Ideally, choices should be designed to encourage you to take decisions that are beneficial for you.

As we found out earlier in this chapter, people can be nudged to reach out for healthy food. When it is accessible and displayed prominently, there is a 28 per cent rise in its consumption. For example, in a school cafeteria, salads and fruits can be kept at eye level and less healthy food further away. Similarly, in your fridge at home, try placing desserts where they are not easily visible and keep healthier options in front.

A cafeteria at Google has this sign: 'People who take big plates tend to eat more'. This has led to an increase in people reaching for smaller plates.

During the pandemic Priyank (author) experimented with creating the right choice architecture for himself. Here is his story:

> *We welcomed our second son into the family just before the lockdown. Confined to the house, I was caught between work and family commitments. With frequent tea and coffee breaks, I began to put on weight despite working out on a treadmill at home. A dietician recommended that I fill my plate only once and eat slowly. I began to resist second helpings and ate with a smaller spoon and fork. It was frustrating but eating slowly improved my satiety. Over the next two months, I lost the weight I had gained.*

These are small ways to trick yourself to ensure the outcomes you want. A colleague flosses her teeth after eating so that she does not snack between meals. A friend wanted to cut down on his evening drink. He knew the urge was greatest in the hour before dinner. To distract himself, he would have a soup or schedule a show to watch on Netflix at that time.

Dan, the psychology professor from earlier in this chapter, conducted an experiment in his consumer behaviour class. In the three sections he was teaching, he set different deadlines for assignments. In the first section, students could choose when to submit their assignments, but once they committed, the deadline was binding on them. In the second section, assignments were due on the last day of the term. For students in the third section, the professor set specific submission dates through the term.

This is how flexibility and choice architecture varied across the three sections.

Section	Instruction	Flexibility	Choice Architecture
1	Students choose the due date	Unlimited, till choice is exercised	Free choice with constraints
2	No due date, anytime before end of semester	Unlimited	Free choice without constraints
3	Each paper due one third way during the term	None	Mandates

Which section do you think had the best results?

Section 3, in which students had the least flexibility, did the best. This was followed by section 1, in which students set their own deadlines. The worst results were in section 2, in which no deadlines were set.

These are some insights from the experiment:

- Deadlines, whether voluntary or externally imposed, lead to better outcomes.
- Even when offered unlimited flexibility, many students recognize their tendency to procrastinate and prefer to pre-commit to a submission date.
- Not having a deadline either externally imposed or through a pre-commitment may appear the most appealing option, but it requires discipline and resolve to work effectively.

Celebrate Small Wins

As McKinsey & Company discovered, small changes can result in substantial outcomes. It is the notion that a butterfly's wings can create tiny changes in the atmosphere that can alter the path of a tornado. Mathematician and meteorologist Edward Lorenz was running a computer programme to predict the weather. One night, Lorenz entered 0.506 rather than 0.506127 into the computer and left for a coffee. When he returned an hour later, the computer had simulated two months of weather data that were entirely different from earlier results.

Initially, Lorenz thought this was an error or a bug in the programme. In fact, the results were different due to a round-off. Lorenz published his findings in a paper called 'Deterministic Nonperiodic Flow'. He sent his findings to another conference and forgot to add a title. A friend called it 'Does the flap of a butterfly's wings in Brazil set off a tornado in Texas?' The metaphor has stuck.

A small win can also generate a sense of satisfaction. As a graduate student, Brad Myers, who is now a faculty member at Carnegie Mellon University, made fellow students run a search on a computer database. Some databases had a progress bar that graphically displayed the extent to which the task had been completed. Even when told that the bar was inaccurate, 86 per cent of the participants preferred to have the progress bar. Myers initially called it a 'per cent done progress indicator'.

We have two reasons to celebrate small wins. First, large wins, with higher stakes and rewards, are likely to be less frequent. Like the proverbial low-hanging fruit, small wins are much easier to achieve. In some cases, performance may also decline when a win involves high rewards.

Second, small wins will build momentum to keep you on track towards a long-term goal. Progress at each step will increase engagement as the end goal becomes clear and is within reach. Video games have progress bars and achievement markers. Gamers can see the extent to which they have completed a task and how close they are to the next level. This motivates them to keep playing.

A small win also encourages a renewed effort for more wins. Alcoholics Anonymous doesn't expect its members to initially give up or abstain from alcohol for the rest of their lives. It's a goal which may not even be comprehensible or within reach to many who need support. Depending on the severity of their addiction, members are encouraged to stay away from alcohol for an hour or a day at a time. These small wins are celebrated and reinforced with calls, meetings, and slogans that provide traction and create momentum to work towards a big goal.

* * *

Teresa Amabile is a professor at Harvard Business School. Along with her co-author Steven Kramer, a developmental psychologist, Amabile wanted to understand how firms promote creativity and productivity among employees. Over a four-month period, they studied white-collar employees working in a variety of industries. At the end of every day, employees answered questions on their motivational levels, their emotions and moods, and feelings about their work environment.

After scrutinizing 12,000 entries, and the personal stories behind them, they found that employees' biggest motivation was a feeling of making progress. This was true even when progress was small. Factors like salary and bonuses, which were assumed to be important, did not figure in the list. In *The Progress Principle*, Amabile and Kramer described how minor events, which may not significantly impact an overall project, have a major effect on how people feel about their work. Small wins boost an individual's inner life balance, which then becomes a source of pride and joy.

An employee working in a software company made this entry in his diary:

> *I smashed that bug that's been frustrating me for almost a calendar week. That may not be an event to you, but I live a very drab life, so I'm all hyped.*

This conclusion is not new. In 1968, Frederick Herzberg published an article 'One More Time: How Do You Motivate Employees?' While Herzberg began by debating the merits of a KITA* management approach, he concluded that people are most satisfied when they experience a sense of achievement in their jobs.

Let's imagine it's a Friday evening and friends have dropped by your place. You use a delivery app to order food. The tracking feature on the app keeps you updated. It informs you that your:

- order has been accepted
- food is under preparation
- delivery person has collected your order
- order is on its way
- order has arrived

Every update is a small step ahead in anticipation of the meal with your friends.

---

* Kick In The Ass.

An old Chinese proverb reminds us of the power of small wins: 'The man who moves a mountain begins by carrying away small stones'.

Engage with Social Groups

Behaviour can travel like a contagion from your friends (one degree), your friends' friends (two degrees), and even from your friends' friends' friends (three degrees) whom you might not even know. These effects can travel both ways, and it is only beyond three degrees that their influence wanes.

Nicholas Christakis is a medical doctor with a PhD in sociology. At Yale University, he has appointments in the Medical School and School of Business, besides others. As a palliative care doctor in Chicago, he was attending to a patient who was dying of dementia. She was being attended to by her daughter who was exhausted from caring for her mother. The daughter's husband was also tired by his wife's exhaustion.

One night Christakis got a call from the daughter's husband's friend who said he was depressed by what was happening to his friend. Can social ties, in which we are all embedded, affect the way we think and behave?

Christakis and his co-author James Fowler decided to study the influence social ties have on our smoking habits, attempts to control weight, and even our overall happiness. They found that having a friend who is obese increases your risk of obesity by 57 per cent.

So the next time you want to give up smoking, remember the statistics. If your spouse gives up smoking, there is a 67 per cent chance that you will also give it up. If a close friend quits, your chances are 36 per cent, and if a sibling stops smoking, the chances that you will follow are 25 per cent.

Another way of describing this phenomenon is social contagion. In *Connected: The Surprising Power of Our Social Networks*, Christakis and Fowler write:

> *How we feel, what we know, whom we marry, whether we fall ill, how much money we make, and whether we vote—all depend on the ties that bind us. Social networks spread happiness, generosity, and love. They are always there exerting subtle and dramatic influences over our choices, actions, thoughts, feelings, even our desires.*

Happiness is contagious. Having a friend who is happy and lives within 1.6 kilometres of you increases the probability of your being happy by 25 per cent. Happy siblings and spouses also make you happy, though their influence is smaller at 14 and 8 per cent, respectively.

If you are waiting for a pay hike, consider this: getting a raise of 10,000 dollars is less likely to make you happy than having a happy friend. In fact, it is better to have a friend, who has a friend, who has a friend who is happy rather than getting that raise.

* * *

Let's see how doctors can be nudged by their social networks.

It is widely known that taking antibiotics too often can lead to antimicrobial resistance (AMR). The United Nations estimates that the death toll due to AMR will reach 10 million by

2050. The chief medical officer in England found some doctors were overprescribing antibiotics. The top 20 per cent of these doctors received a letter informing them that 80 per cent of their colleagues prescribed fewer antibiotics. Antibiotic prescriptions dropped by 3.3 per cent. This may not seem much, until you realize that the nudge resulted in 75,000 fewer prescriptions across 800 practices.

Think of your closest friends. Ask yourself:

- What is important to them?
- How do they spend their leisure time?
- How happy are their families?

They could be nudging you. Just as, without their knowing, you too could be nudging them.

Dark Side of Nudging

Scott Stevens had a master's degree in business and finance and earned a six-figure salary. He owned three cars and had two country club memberships. Even his daughters' college tuitions were covered by his benefits package.

Scott, however, had recently lost his job. One morning in August 2012 he told his wife, Stacy, that he was going for an interview. Scott, as he usually did, packed an apple and a sandwich for his lunch. Then he drove to a casino in West Virginia to play his favourite slot machine.

Four hours later, he mailed Stacy a five-page letter. It had a cheque for 4,000 dollars, the amount left in his account after gambling. It also had instructions on how Stacy could avoid responsibility for his losses. Scott then drove to the high school where his children once studied and texted his wife and three daughters identical messages: 'I love you'.

Next, Scott dialled 911 and told the operator he was going to kill himself. A few hours later, three police officers arrived at the Stevens' home. That was when Stacy learned of her husband's suicide.

Scott got his first taste of gambling in 2006 at a trade show in Las Vegas. He later won a jackpot and became addicted to gambling. To feed his addiction, Scott gradually embezzled four million dollars from his company account. When it was discovered, Scott lost his job.

Are gamblers being nudged to behave irrationally?

Studies on the design and algorithms used in slot machines suggest so. These machines can generate half of a casino's revenue. The West Virginia casino Scott frequented had 1,500 slot machines placed close together. When someone wins, the jingles in these machines are loud and celebratory. This attracts everyone's attention and creates a false sense of euphoria.

Two types of nudges are especially worrying: a near miss and a loss disguised as a win.

To win, the three reels on a slot machine must match. Often, only two match and the third stops just above or below the pay line. Players respond to a near miss with  excitement, more persistent play, and higher bets. Studies find that players react to near misses and wins very similarly. Slot machines are often programmed to offer a near miss more often than can happen by random chance. Near-miss events nudge players to continue gambling even when they are no longer enjoying it.

Another way to nudge gamblers is to disguise a loss as a win. In many casinos traditional slot machines have been replaced with electronic ones that have up to 100 lines per spin. In addition to a straight line, players can bet on multiple outcomes and invariably win some combination on every spin. The winnings, however, are less than the amount they have bet. Despite this, loud celebratory sounds deceive players into believing they have won, leading many to overestimate their wins. Among novice players both a win and a loss disguised as a win result in elevated skin conductance and diffused activity in the region of the brain associated with reward and reinforcement.

Gamblers often believe that they win on slot machines with their skills. Imagine you are a basketball player practising free throws. You try various techniques to gradually get the ball closer to the hoop. The probability of succeeding increases with every subsequent throw. This is deliberate practice, which we explored in Chapter 1. In gambling, however, a player has a random chance of a win in every round.

Let's return to Scott's story. After her husband's death, Stacy sued the casino and the slot machine manufacturer, accusing them of exploiting casino patrons. Stacy's legal counsel argued that slot machines manipulate the human mind to produce a trance like state in which gamblers cannot take balanced decisions.

Stacy lost the case in court.

Thaler, the Nobel Prize winning economist at the start of this chapter, always adds 'Nudge for good', while signing his book.

So What?

The following anecdotes highlight how our students nudged themselves to exercise, eat healthy food, play a musical instrument, and complete an online course.

Ayesha* has a large desk calendar on her table at work. Every time she goes for a run, Ayesha crosses the date with a red marker. The mark is big and bold. Even if she's feeling lazy or tired on a particular day, Ayesha ends up going for a run so that she can keep crossing out dates.

As he gradually put on weight, Piyush realized he needed to stop indulging in his high-calorie diet. He started eating lunch with Mihika, a fitness freak. Watching her order smoothies and salads, he began making healthier choices. Piyush also joined a gym near his office and began to work out at least twice a week.

Mohit was learning to play the guitar but couldn't find time to practise. Working remotely from home, he kept the guitar next to his desk. Every time he took a break, rather than scrolling through his social media feed, Mohit would strum a tune on his guitar.

For two years, Radhika postponed signing up for an online course that could help her career. One day she shared this intention on social media. On her profile she included the course certification, along with 'in progress' in smaller font. Fear of losing face among family and friends nudged Radhika to complete the course and get certified.

We too had to nudge ourselves to finish this book, the idea for which had been brewing for a long time. A colleague facetiously enquired whether we were on our second, or maybe

---

* Our students' names have been changed to protect their identity.

third, volume. Of course, we had good reasons for the delay: teaching commitments, research deadlines, and then the pandemic. We began setting targets for each other's work and committed to our publisher to have the manuscript ready by a particular date.

Let's return to the opening story of the fly in the men's room at Amsterdam's Schiphol Airport.

We heard back from a student who remembered the class. He had used a public toilet in Tokyo in which the urinal had been set up as a game. An LCD screen calculated the user's accuracy.

As a nudge, should the user's display screen be positioned inside or outside the toilet?

3

BE INTELLECTUALLY HUMBLE

we are all confident idiots

謙遜

"Be like the bamboo
the higher you grow
the deeper you bow"
–Chinese Proverb

It is 2004.

You are on Route 101 driving from San Francisco to Palo Alto. On the highway a billboard has a puzzle you think you can solve. When you get home, you log on to the website and enter your answer.

A few seconds go by.

Your answer is correct.

Another question pops up on the screen, then another. After answering several of them, you are redirected to Google's home page and invited to upload your resume.

A few weeks later, you are being interviewed at Googleplex, Mountain View. The interviewer asks:

- How many golf balls can fit in an airplane?
- How many cows does Canada have?
- Why are manhole covers round?
- How many times a day do a clock's hands overlap?

Getting a job at Google is tougher than being admitted to Harvard Business School.* In 2019, Google hired 6,600 people

---

* Harvard Business School has a 9 per cent acceptance rate.

from 3.3 million applications. However, human resource managers at Google soon realized that brainteasers only make the interviewer look smart. They are no longer used during interviews.

What do you need to get a job at Google?

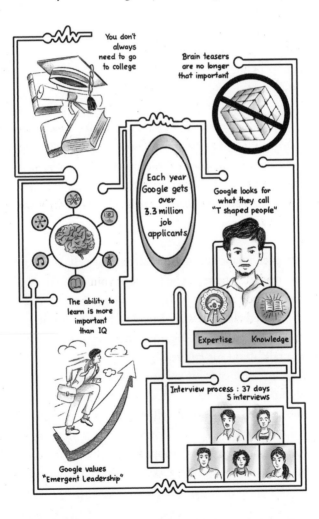

Laszlo Bock was Head of People Operations at Google for a decade. He says it is not only grades. Your ability to perform at work is unrelated to your college performance as the skills you need in your job are very different.

What is Google looking for?

More than IQ, Google values the ability to learn, especially from your failures.

Can you cultivate it?

Yes, by being intellectually humble.

Laszlo says:

> *Without intellectual humility, you are unable to learn. It's feeling the sense of ownership to step in and the humility to step back and embrace the better ideas of others . . . we have a strong bias against leaders who champion themselves; people who use 'I' far more often than 'we'.*

This chapter is about intellectual humility. It is linked to a growth mindset, where you believe that your capabilities depend on your attitude and effort. It is also about how you deal with failure. Basketball superstar Michael Jordan admits missing 9,000 shots and losing 300 games. Why would a sports legend like him talk about his failures?

Educator and content creator Ankur Warikoo has a list of everything he tried and failed at. After completing her PhD, Melanie applied for several fellowships. When they were all rejected, she wrote a failure resume about herself. It was the same year Ronaldinho was dropped from the Brazilian national football team. There is a connection between these two stories.

Does your body posture affect how you think and feel? Can you be so ignorant that you don't realize how ignorant you are? Is it possible to have a big ego and a small ego at the same time?

This chapter answers these and other questions.

Are You Intellectually Humble?

Which of these statements is true about you?

1. I accept that my beliefs and attitudes may be wrong.
2. I reconsider my opinions when presented with new evidence.
3. I recognize value in opinions that differ from my own.
4. I question my opinions, positions, and viewpoints because they could be wrong.
5. I seek information that differs from what I already think is true.

Give yourself one point for a 'no' answer, two for 'sometimes', and three for 'yes'.

If you score over nine, you are intellectually humble. Ideally, people who are intellectually humble say 'yes' to all 5 statements and score 15 points.

You can cultivate intellectual humility by adopting a growth mindset. A mindset is a lens, a type of filter that helps you make sense of everything around you. Much of our understanding of mindsets comes from the work of Stanford University psychologist Carol Dweck.

People with a fixed mindset believe that intelligence is innate and cannot be changed. They prefer doing things they are good at and avoid those that portray them negatively. In contrast, those with a growth mindset like being challenged. They enjoy learning by trying new things even if they don't succeed at first. Failure is an opportunity to grow rather than something to be feared. In a growth mindset the focus is on the process rather than on the result.

Recruiters at Google look for 'Googleyness', which is difficult to define but easy to spot. Laszlo describes it as consisting of:

> *Attributes like fun, a certain dose of intellectual humility (it's hard to learn if you can't admit that you might be wrong), a strong measure of conscientiousness (we want owners not employees), and comfort and ambiguity.*

Interviews at Google often begin with statements like:

- Tell me about a time when you failed
- Tell me about a time when you took charge of a project beyond your expertise and knowledge
- Tell me about a time when you overcame adversity

The University of Hong Kong (HKU), described as the 'Harvard of Asia' and the 'Oxbridge of East Asia', is known for its academic rigour. All classes are in English, which is not the first language of many of its students. A group of students in the social sciences were told that knowledge of English was very important for academic success. They were then given an English proficiency test. Along with their scores, they were offered a free course to improve their language skills.

You would expect most students to sign up for the course. Researchers, however, found that only those with a growth mindset, who believed that intelligence is malleable, opted for it.

Dweck says:

> *Students who hold a fixed view of their intelligence care so much about looking smart that they act dumb. What could be dumber than giving up a chance to learn something that is essential for your own success?*

After failing at something, a person with a fixed mindset will say, 'I can't do this'. Those with a growth mindset add a three-letter word at the end of the sentence.

Can you guess the word?

YET.

I can't do this *yet*.

While mentoring our students, we find the use of the right language can build a growth mindset. Using the word 'yet' is one way to develop it. It implies that you are working towards a goal and will need effort and time to get there.

How can we encourage students to adopt a growth mindset?

Think of a school report card. Rather than the usual pass or fail, suppose the teacher could give a student a *not yet* grade. Would that motivate a child who had failed to try harder the next time?

This grading rubric was tested at a Chicago school. Dweck found that despite failing, children felt that they were on a learning curve. The teacher also made children recite: 'The brain is like a muscle, the more you use it, the stronger it will become'.

Can you change your mindset?

Mindsets are beliefs, albeit powerful ones. We have both types of mindsets residing in us. Transitioning from one mindset to the other is a gradual process. It is a journey, not a destination. Just being aware, and constantly reminded, of the power of a growth mindset can change the way you think and influence your decisions.

Now that you are aware of the power of a growth mindset, revisit the statements on intellectual humility from earlier in this chapter. Then get a friend who knows you well to fill them up on your behalf.

Are the scores the same?

Your friend's perception of you, and the way you think of yourself, may differ. Understanding the reason for this will prompt you to make small changes that can alter your mindset.

Assess your attitude towards risk and the way you deal with failure. Remember failure is not a reflection of your ability, it is just a signal that you need to persist and try again.

A Resume of Your Failures

> *I have missed more than 9,000 shots in my career. I have lost almost 300 games. Twenty-six times, I've been trusted to take the game-winning shot and missed. I've failed over and over again in my life. And that is why I succeed.*

This was Michael Jordan in a Nike commercial. He doesn't like his success being attributed to talent or luck.

Why would anyone want to talk about their failures?

To answer that, let's go back to 2010, a year Brazilian football fans will not easily forget. Ronaldinho had just been dropped from the national team for the FIFA World Cup.

Melanie Stefan also remembers that year. After a PhD in biomedical Sciences, Melanie had been applying for fellowships. That day she received yet another rejection.

How did Melanie react?

Cool, I am like Ronaldinho.

Melanie went on to become a computational neuroscientist. Recalling her early rejections, she wrote an article in *Nature,* a top-ranking journal, wondering why we always build a narrative of our successes but gloss over our failures. After all, every goal Ronaldinho missed was available for public viewing. Even his exclusion from the World Cup squad was extensively analysed on social media.

If you were an aspiring sportsperson or a scientist, it would be reassuring to know that even successful people struggle and often fail.

* * *

Ankur remembers his father crying when he didn't clear the IIT entrance exam. After a year at college, Ankur tried again:

Didn't make it, not even close. This time no one cried, not even me. Maybe I knew it all along.

After graduating, Ankur decided to pursue a master's degree. Of the seven universities he applied to, Michigan State University was the only one that accepted him. Following his master's,

Ankur enrolled in a PhD programme. He soon dropped out and returned to India. Unsure of what to do next, Ankur joined the Indian School of Business, Hyderabad.

This is Ankur's failure resume.

Ankur Warikoo
My Failure Resume

I am extremely grateful to be where I am in life. But there were several moments when I wasn't.
It is so easy for us to take our failures seriously and consider them the end of the road. I am the biggest proof that self-doubt exists, and I am equally the best proof that one can overcome it – it's just a battle that never stops.

Inspired by Johannes HausHofer's CV of Failures, I share mine below. With the hope that people realize their problems and challenges are similar to everyone else's. What may be the reaction to it. Or their acceptance in the first place.

At the end of the day, when you undress yourself, the scars tell a story that only you know of
Don't wish for more scars
But be surely aware of the ones you have
Perhaps one day you will be proud of them as well

Schools I Did Not Get Into

1998	Did not clear IIT JEE / AIEEE
	None of the IITs, NITs
	Did not score enough to get through St. Stephen's Physics
	Failed the St. Stephen's Computer Science Interview
1999	Did not clear IITs in the second attempt as well
2001	Failed the IIT Delhi MS Physics Entrance Exam
	Failed the IIT Kanpur MS Physics Interview
2002	Did not get an admit into the PhD Physics Program of Princeton, UC Berkeley, University of Michigan, MIT
2004	Did not get into MBA at IIM Ahmedabad, Bangalore, Calcutta
	(Applied through the NRI GMAT route)
2005	Did not score enough to get interview calls to MBA at IIM Ahmedabad, Bangalore, Calcutta
	(Applied through the CAT)

Corporate Roles I Did Not Get

2004	Citibank Analytics
	Convergys BPO
	This was when I came from the US with an MS in Physics. Just had to get a job, so applied randomly to 11 companies. Never heard back from any. The above called for an interview but never heard back.
2006	Boston Consulting Group
	Citibank
	Deutsche Bank
	MBA Placements - interviewed with the above. Applied to 7 companies beyond this but none of them shortlisted my profile - McKinsey, Google, Tishman Speyer, Goldman Sachs, Accenture, Infosys.
2010	Google
	Facebook
	Post Accentium, I knew I wanted to be within the internet space. Thought PM roles would be best opportunity to learn. But they wanted someone from a technical background.

Investors That Said No (for all the right reasons, or so I think!)

2010	Indian Angel Network
	Mumbai Angels
	9 HNIs
	This was for a startup idea in the food space. Biggest reason – no relevant experience
2015	Lightspeed Ventures, Saif, Matrix Partners, Helion
	While pulling off the Management Buyout of Groupon India

Other failures in life

- Used to enjoy coding in school. Gave it up, for no reason whatsoever
- Have not been able to gift my parents a vacation to the US, for 5 years now
- Whenever my son draws me, I always have a mobile phone in my hand
- I am not an expert at anything. Nothing!

After his MBA, Ankur accepted a batchmate's offer to be a co-founder in his company. A year later, he was fired. He says his friend did the right thing. Ankur and his wife then decided to start a food company but could not raise the capital to fund it.

In 2011, Ankur became the founding CEO of Groupon in India. Four years later, the company decided to exit the country. Ankur offered to buy Groupon's business with capital he intended to raise. Of the 23 venture capitalists he pitched to, 22 rejected him. He manged the buyout only to lose Rs 110 million in the first month. While laying off 80 employees, Ankur cried and apologized to them. It was not their fault; he had failed them.

Attempting to raise funds again, Ankur approached 68 investors. One investor agreed, only to later withdraw the offer. The founders took a cut in salary, while Ankur managed on his credit cards. For his sister's wedding, Ankur raised a loan by offering his parents' home as collateral.

It was to get worse.

Ankur sold his wife's jewellery to buy his son a bicycle. Seeing the birthday present, his son broke down.

Ankur remembers that day:

We broke down too. It was a very difficult moment to realize that you had gotten to this point where you didn't even have money to keep your kids happy.

It took eight years for his new venture 'nearbuy.com' to turn cash positive. Ankur eventually stepped down as CEO, with the other two founders taking over.

It was no different now:

I had no money, no plan, no direction—nothing whatsoever. Exactly where I was 10 years back at 29.

Ankur is now a blogger on social media. In January 2022, he had 50 million views on YouTube. A motivational speaker and storyteller, Ankur likes to share the journey of his failures.

Building Blocks of Intellectual Humility

There are three pillars supporting intellectual humility: having a big and a small ego at the same time, being able to listen to contrary ideas and accepting limits to what you know.

Have a Big and Small Ego

Imagine being in a job interview. You had prepared well and were confident, yet it didn't work out as you expected.

Could your body posture have influenced how you thought and performed?

Non-verbal displays, such as your posture, can give you a sense of power. At least that's what Dana Carney, Amy Cuddy, and Andy Yap found in a study on power posing. They took their cue from the animal kingdom where expansive postures are a sign of dominance.

Dana, a psychologist and professor at UC Berkeley, noticed that though her women students were academically at par with the men, they didn't do as well during class discussions. Many women would sit in low-power poses, wrapping their ankles around each other or supporting their elbows in their palms.

In a study, Dana and her co-authors divided participants into two groups. One group was assigned high-power poses and the other low-power ones. Participants held two poses for a minute each and reported how powerful they felt.

Their testosterone and cortisol levels were taken, and their risk-taking ability was measured with a gambling game.* The authors concluded that power posing boosts self-confidence and performance. Simply put, body language has a physiological and psychological influence on behaviour.

This research was published and quickly became popular. Amy featured on talk shows and travelled the world on speaking engagements. Playing on the adage 'Fake it till you make it', Amy told her followers,

---

* Each participant was given two dollars and had the option to either keep the money (safe bet) or choose to roll a die for a payoff for either zero or four dollars (risky bet).

'Fake it till you *become* it'. With 20 million views, her TED Talk is among the most popular in the channel's history. Power posing became a rage.

So, the next time you are about to ask for a raise, should you spend a few minutes in front of the mirror holding a 'Wonder Woman' pose?

Wait, there is more to the story.

Subsequent research has not validated these results. Many social scientists have even discredited power posing as a pseudoscience. As the controversy snowballed, Dana, the first author in the study, changed her stance:

> *As evidence has come in over these past 2+ years, my views have updated to reflect the evidence. As such, I do not believe that 'power pose' effects are real.*

Would you publicly retract your professional work after it has been widely recognized?

Dana's act of accepting errors and limitations required intellectual humility. Since then, she has worked on studies that have examined similar phenomena and reached different conclusions.

In contrast, Amy, who was the second author of the paper, continues to propagate power posing and has even written a book on it. Lack of scientific support for power posing has made Amy the target of widespread criticism on social media. This has hurt her reputation and even affected her health.

As the controversy unfolded *The New York Times* described Amy's state:

> *She stopped taking calls and went almost completely offline. She found she couldn't eat: at 5-foot-5 in, Amy went down to 100 pounds (45 kgs).*

In 2017, Amy left her tenure-track position at Harvard Business School.

Dana is not alone in updating her position when presented with new or contrary evidence. The editors of *Nature* and *Science*, both well respected journals in their fields, decided to review articles they had previously published. They found that 33 per cent of the studies could not be replicated. This upheaval led to a 'Loss of Confidence Project', which encourages scholars to question the theory and methodology underlying their research and accept responsibility for conclusions that cannot be supported using newer methods.

Like scholars and scientists, we must be willing to acknowledge that we can be wrong. For Laszlo, the head of Google's People Operations whom we met earlier in the chapter, this is an important part of being intellectually humble:

> *[Successful people will] be zealots about their point of view. But then you say, 'here's a new fact' and they go 'oh well, that changes things; you are right'. You need a big ego and a small ego in the same person at the same time.*

Listen to Contrary Ideas

Two childhood friends are having a drink at a bar in Alaska. One is a priest and the other an atheist. They are debating the existence of God.

Priest: So, you still don't believe that the Almighty exists?

Atheist: Look, it's not like I have not given God a chance. I even tried the prayer thing. It didn't work.

Priest: Did you really pray? When did that happen?

Atheist: Just last month.
The priest looks at his friend with surprise.

Atheist: I was caught in a terrible blizzard. I was totally lost and couldn't see a thing. It was twenty degrees below zero. I fell to my knees and cried out, 'Oh God, if there is a God! I am lost in this blizzard. I am going to die if you don't help me'.

Priest: Well, you must believe in God now. After all, here you are . . . alive.

Atheist: No, that's not how it happened. A couple of Eskimos came wandering by and showed me the way back to camp.

Both smiled, each bemused by the other's dogmatic perspective.

* * *

This is an example of a confirmation bias, in which we seek, interpret, and even recall information that confirms our point of view. We like to think of ourselves as being consistent. Conflicting views, attitudes, and behaviours make us uncomfortable. We often

choose to interpret information in a way that supports our viewpoint while ignoring contradictory evidence.

* * *

Have you wondered how people select the books they buy and read?

In Chapter 2, sociologists Christakis and Fowler found that obesity, smoking, and even happiness can spread through networks. Valdis Krebs, a network researcher, mapped people who purchased books on politics from Barnes & Noble and Amazon. Using Amazon's feature 'Customers who bought this book also bought these books', he found that most buyers preferred to engage with books that reinforced their thinking. During the 2008 US presidential campaign, for example, Democrats and Republicans bought books that supported their ideology.

The map also featured a few books that both sides bought. What were these buyers doing?

They were challenging themselves with a contrary point of view. They wanted to be better informed and understand another viewpoint. Some of them may have even held two opposing perspectives at the same time.

Think about it. By engaging with a contradictory perspective, you might discover that some aspects of it are reasonable. Even if you not convinced by the contrary view, you will still benefit by being able to refute it better. Either way, your arguments are likely to be sharper and your position more nuanced.

Why are we so sensitive to a view different from our own?

Neuroscientists tell us that when faced with opposing views, the part of our brain associated with identity experiences increased activity. The brain feels threatened by information that challenges our belief system. It then responds as if it faces a physical threat.

When challenged with a contrary view, people who are intellectually humble will:

- treat the contradiction as *food for thought*,
- encourage constructive conflict by *daring to disagree*, and
- seek people with *alternate ways of thinking*.

Let's see an example of this.

It is the 1950s. Alice Stewart, an epidemiologist and physician, practises in the UK. The first woman to be admitted to both the Association of Physicians and the Royal College of Physicians, Alice is outgoing and popular, with a wide social circle.

Alice's collaborator, George Kneale, is just the opposite. He is a statistician who prefers the company of numbers. Tall and heavyset, George avoids eye contact with others and challenges everything Alice does. He questions the models Alice uses, her data-crunching methods, and any position she takes.

Alice and George constantly debate and engage in constructive criticism to sharpen their thinking. George seeks to create conflict:

My job is to prove Dr [Alice] Stewart wrong.

Alice, in turn, has the confidence that if George is unable to prove her wrong, she must be right.

Alice is investigating the increase in childhood cancers. At this time, most diseases are connected with poverty. Alice, however, finds that even healthy children are being diagnosed with cancer. She wants to resolve this anomaly, but funding her research is a challenge.

Alice gets a grant of 1,000 pounds from the Lady Tata Memorial Fund. She is virtually looking for the proverbial needle in the haystack and, given her limited budget, will have only one chance to collect data. Alice and George put together a wide variety of questions for the parents:

- Did the children eat boiled sweets or consume coloured drinks?
- Does their home have indoor or outdoor plumbing?
- At what age did the children begin school?
- Did the children eat fish and chips?

The study does not find any connection between poverty and cancer. Rather, it finds that X-rays on pregnant woman are responsible for leukaemia in children.

Unfortunately, the medical community vehemently refutes these findings. X-rays are considered a miracle in medical diagnosis and therapy. Alice's results contradict the accepted view that low dosages of radiation are harmless. Alice is ostracized from the research community and denied further funding for her work.

It takes more than 20 years for the scientific community to acknowledge her results and end the practice of prenatal X-rays. Even today, as you enter a radiology clinic, you will see this sign.

Accept Limits to What You Know

Have you ever tried to send a secret message?

Try writing on a paper with lemon juice. Only when the paper is heated and turns brown does the writing become visible. That's why lemon juice is called 'invisible ink'.

In 1995, McArthur Wheeler, a resident of Pittsburgh, robbed two local banks. He didn't disguise himself or even wear a mask. In fact, he smiled directly into the surveillance cameras. McArthur was not a small man; at five feet six inches, he weighed 122 kgs. Within an hour, the police were at McArthur's home. When shown the surveillance footage, McArthur mumbled in disbelief:

But I wore the juice.

After hearing from a friend about invisible ink, McArthur rubbed lemon juice on his face. As abundant precaution he then took a picture of himself with a Polaroid camera. The photograph was blank. Maybe McArthur had used defective film or not adjusted the camera properly. It was also possible that the camera was pointed in the wrong direction.

The *Pittsburgh Post-Gazette* carried the story of the lemon juice robber. David Dunning, a social psychologist and professor at Cornell University, read the article. McArthur was clearly too ignorant to be a bank robber. Dunning wondered if McArthur was *too ignorant to know that he was too ignorant* to be a bank robber.

Along with his student Justin Kruger, Dunning decided to explore this further. In one study, participants were exposed to technical words used in politics, biology, physics, and geography. In addition to genuine subject-related vocabulary, some made-up terms had been inserted. Nearly 90 per cent of the participants claimed to have some knowledge about the invented jargon. This false sense of confidence is called the Dunning–Kruger effect:

> *Incompetence does not leave people disoriented, perplexed, or cautious. Instead, the incompetent are often blessed with an inappropriate confidence.*

How do you make people realize that they don't know as much as they think they do?

Make them do a toilet test. In a study, volunteers were asked to rate their level of understanding of a flush toilet. They were then made to write a detailed step-by-step account of how it worked. After that, they read an expert's description of its working.

When asked to rate their understanding a second time, participants were less confident about their knowledge. The complexity of a flush toilet became apparent to them. This fallacy is known as the 'illusion of explanatory depth'. With their confidence at more reasonable levels, participants began to ask questions about how a toilet actually worked.

When we engage with a new field, we initially have a false sense of confidence. Soon, the field's complexity, and our own lack of knowledge, become clear. Ideally this should make us recalibrate our confidence to a more reasonable level. Our confidence might even fall as we wonder if the field is beyond our understanding. However, as we study the field, our knowledge and confidence increase.

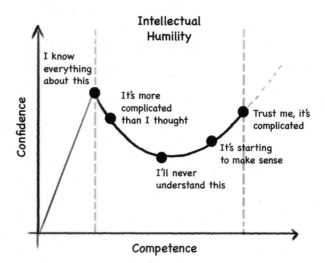

Intellectual humility lies at the centre of the Dunning–Kruger curve. To paraphrase the aphorist* William Feather, intellectual humility is the fine line between knowing what you know and knowing what you don't know.

So What?

> *People who are right a lot, listen a lot,*
> *and they change their mind a lot.*
> *If you don't change your mind frequently,*
> *you're going to be wrong a lot.*
> —Jeff Bezos, Chairman, Amazon

---

* Someone who is known to compose or use aphorisms, i.e., pithy expressions of a general truth or expression.

This is a personal vignette about Mukesh (author).

At 42, I finally began a PhD programme. My wife and I had long planned and discussed this transition during evening walks in the park. After being an entrepreneur for two decades I would be a student again. My friends and family felt that this 'new flirtation' would not last long.

The first hurdle was the Common Admission Test (CAT). It had taken a year of preparation and two failed attempts at CAT for the PhD committee to consider my application. The institute's website favoured candidates with a research profile. Fortunately, that year, Babson College and the London Business School included India in their global survey on entrepreneurship. IIM Bangalore was selected as the country partner. Despite a lack of familiarity with statistics or data collection, I volunteered and was accepted for the project. I later learnt that the committee debated how a candidate of my age would manage the rigours of many years of research.

A few weeks after the term began, we had an operations research quiz. The professor put up the marks outside his office door. The class average was 11 out of 30. I scored four. A meeting with the teaching assistant did not go well. I met the professor, who insisted that even the four marks had been given gratuitously. He was patient; after all, I was older than him.

My first reaction was to quietly return home. The unusual study schedule was a good excuse. Most courses required group work, and 'all-nighters' were the norm. Another pretext could be that my company needed me back. Continuing with the programme carried a risk. After the first year, students who did not make the cut-off would be dropped. Their names would be widely known.

Younger course-mates in the MBA cohort had a different mindset. They viewed it as a challenge. Remember the psychologist Carol Dweck and 'I can't do it *yet*' from earlier in this chapter? My new friends felt test scores would improve and merely reflected being away from a classroom for many years. I doubted it.

Given the loss of face in leaving the programme, I decided to carry on. I moved into student housing with its common toilets and shared living spaces. I realized that the quantitative courses would be the most challenging. The class directory had the names of students who were from the same university I had attended. I asked to be in their groups. The fact that I had studied at our common alma mater when they were not yet born was not lost on them.* A few even offered to tutor me the night before a test.

During the first year of the programme, there were few trips off campus, except to take my new friends home for beer and dinner. The all-night study sessions continued. Other students in the dormitory gradually tolerated the 'older man' living in their midst.

Test and quiz scores began to improve. The final grade in operations was a C. By the time the MBA cohort graduated, I had completed all my coursework. Two challenges remained: a day-long comprehensive exam and writing a dissertation.

With some intellectual humility, both got done.

---

* While introducing me one batchmate said, 'Mr Sud and I are from the same institute. When he studied there though, I was just a gleam in my parents' eyes'.

4

DANCE WITH DISCIPLINES

when ideas have sex

Have you seen a frog fly?

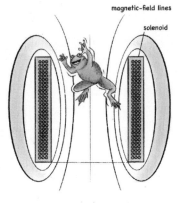

magnetic-field lines

solenoid

Andre Geim, a physicist, won an Ig Nobel Prize for making a frog float in air.

Magnets attract and repel ferromagnetic materials. Water is weakly ferromagnetic. When a frog, whose body is 75 per cent water, is exposed to a high-intensity magnetic field, it levitates. Don't worry, our smiling frog was not harmed in the experiment.

Many of Andre's colleagues thought the flying frog was an April Fool's prank. Once confirmed to be true, Andre received several requests, including one from the UK. The head of a religious group there wanted to levitate in front of his congregation. He offered a million pounds for this.

The Ig Nobel prize is awarded for scientific achievements that initially make people laugh and then think again. In 2011, a Japanese team invented a wasabi smoke detector for the hearing impaired. Made in partnership with a perfume manufacturer, the device emits a pungent, wasabi-like smell on sensing a fire. It was tested on 14 volunteers. Within two minutes of the detector being activated, 13 of them woke up; the 14th volunteer had a blocked nose.

Researchers at the National Institute of Mental Health and Neurosciences (NIMHANS), Bangalore, won an Ig Nobel for discovering that rhinotillexomania is common among adolescents.[*]

---

[*] A condition of picking one's nose endlessly.

In 2002, mathematicians from the College of Veterinary Sciences in Kerala received the prize for estimating the total surface area of Indian elephants. They spent three years measuring elephants from the Gemini Circus, the local forest department, and a temple. Their formula could predict the surface area of both male and female elephants of different age groups and body weights. This later became a quiz question on a television show. Contestants were asked to name the most foolish research study from Kerala. This was the one.

The Ig Nobel award ceremony is held at Harvard University every year. Permission is sought before announcing the winners' names as many researchers may not like to list this achievement on their resumes. Researchers tend to select a field of scholarship early in their careers and spend their professional life studying it.

Andre has a different approach:

> *I do not dig deep, I graze shallow . . . I don't want to carry on studying something from cradle to grave. The biggest adventure is to move into areas where you are not an expert. Sometimes I joke that I am not interested in doing re-search only search.*

Andre's research extends across several fields. He observed geckos walking upside down on a ceiling and along walls. With his colleagues, Andre invented gecko tape. It synthesizes setae—a type of bristle—that mimics the microscopic hair under a gecko's feet. One day, he hopes, this will help humans scale buildings. Just like Spiderman.

Andre dances with disciplines.

Has this affected his professional reputation? Is he taken less seriously by fellow researchers in the scientific community?

Thomson-Reuters named Andre one of the most active scientists in the world and a pioneer in the fields of diamagnetic levitation, gecko tape, and graphene. For his work on graphene, Andre and his colleagues were awarded the 2010 Nobel Prize. His acceptance speech was titled 'Random Walk to Graphene'. Andre values both his Ig Nobel and Nobel prizes equally.

Can dancing with disciplines solve problems in the real world?

Manjul Bhargava is one of the youngest tenured professors at Princeton University. His interest in music and poetry helped him win a Fields Medal in mathematics.* This chapter will explore how intermingling of ideas can sprout fresh ones. It was this belief that encouraged a boy born in a remote village in Pakistan to one day acquire TED Talks.

Dancing with disciplines has three underlying pillars: building a T-shaped profile, exploring a liberal education and acting as a deliberate amateur. They will help you think differently and discover new insights and knowledge.

Interdisciplinary thinking is not new. During World War II, Germany used the Enigma code to communicate with their U-boats patrolling the Atlantic Ocean. To break Enigma, the Allies assembled a team of experts from a range of disciplines to work together to decrypt it.

To be a codebreaker with the Allies, you would have to solve a crossword in less than 12 minutes. The crossword appeared in *The Daily Telegraph* on 13 January 1942.

Try it later in this chapter.

---

* This is considered the highest honour in mathematics and equivalent to a Nobel Prize.

Maths, Music, and Sanskrit

Mira Bhargava, a mathematics professor at Hofstra University, found that the only way to keep her three-year-old son still was by challenging him with maths problems. Manjul had a very intuitive way of solving them. Rather than using a pencil and paper, Manjul would move his fingers back and forth in the air while deep in thought.

Manjul was often bored with his school curriculum. Mira would then take him along to her maths classes. Much to the amusement of Mira's students, Manjul once corrected his mother while solving a probability problem on the board.

When Mira returned from shopping, Manju would try and heap all the oranges together. He wondered if there was a formula for the number of oranges that could be stacked in a pyramid. The eight-year-old finally figured it out.

$N \times (N+1) \times (N+2)/6$

Every few years, Mira took Manjul to India to visit his grandfather, a Sanskrit scholar. During these visits, Manjul would listen to classical music, learn Sanskrit poetry, and hear tales of ancient Indian mathematicians. Later, as an undergraduate at Harvard University, Manjul completed the required eight courses needed to major in mathematics. The 27 others he chose were in Sanskrit, classical music, and computer science.

Manjul likes to surround himself with Rubik's cubes, Zometool, and other puzzles. Playing with toys and walking around in nature helped him find an elegant solution to a problem that had eluded mathematicians for centuries. Manjul imagined placing numbers at the four corners of a mini cube and then cutting it in half. The Bhargava Cube, as his discovery is known, was a reformation of the Gauss method of composing quadratic forms. This later formed part of Manjul's PhD dissertation.

Manjul thinks of mathematics differently:

> *Mathematics is very much a playful experience . . .*
> *one key to solve hard mathematical problems that*
> *people have been thinking about for many years is to*
> *think about them in a totally different way.*

Growing up, Manjul played the sitar and violin. He learned the tabla from his mother and later from Pandit Prem Prakash Sharma and Ustad Zakir Hussain. In the fall of 2005, Manjul persuaded Zakir to spend a semester at Princeton, where Manjul was teaching. They both co-taught 'Introduction to Music', which was the most popular course offered by the music department that semester.

Manjul has performed at Central Park in New York City. At Princeton, he collaborated with Dan Truman, a pianist and assistant professor of music. Rehearsing for a concert, Dan thought Manjul was a professional tabla player. The third member of the group was a professor in the computer science department.

Manjul likens his field of number theory to patterns in nature and sequences in music. For him music and mathematics are forms of art in different languages. Manjul feels these disciplines, along with poetry, can help us understand truths about ourselves and the world we live in.

At a seminar in a Bengaluru high school, he spoke about the two syllables in Sanskrit poetry: unstressed (short syllables of one beat) and stressed (long syllables of two beats).

He asked the audience:

> *Suppose you have 8 beats left in the poetry that you're composing . . . How many ways can you fill that in with long syllables and short syllables?*

In the language of poets, how many meters are there in *n* beats of long and short syllables?

There are four possible answers:

- long (2)-long(2)-long(2)-long(2)
- [short(1)-short(1)] x 4
- short(1)-long(2)-long(2)-long (2)-short(1)
- short(1)-long(2)-short(1)-short(1)-long(2)-short(1)

Sanskrit scholar Hemachandra (1050 CE) had proposed beginning a sequence by writing down the numbers 1 and 2. Each subsequent number is the sum of the previous two. The *n*th digit is the number of rhythms with *n* beats.

So, the sequence is:

1, 2, 3, 5, 8, 13, 21, 34, 55, 89 . . .

You can have 34 rhythms for the same poem without missing a beat (*taal*). This is the Hemachandra number sequence. It is also known as the Fibonacci sequence, after the Italian mathematician (1170 CE) who discovered it much later. Hemachandra numbers feature in poetry, visual arts, architecture, and even in nature. The pattern of seeds at the centre of a sunflower follows this sequence. So do the number of spirals from the centre of a pine cone to the outside edge. Next time you see a sunflower or find a pine cone, check it yourself.

Manjul says that even maths and magic have common roots. He offers a freshman course 'The Mathematics of Magic Tricks and Games'. It draws students from all backgrounds and academic levels. In some assignments, students flip through a deck of cards to acquaint themselves with mathematical principles in games and magic tricks.

Manjul and the physicist Andre are not alone in their desire to connect disparate disciplines.

Unboxing Disciplines

> *Most of us have tunnel vision . . . there is unbelievable inspiration and wisdom to be gained from listening to people well outside your field. The breakthrough spark often comes from outside the little box in which you're focused.*
>
> —Chris Anderson

It was 1984.

A conference on technology, entertainment, and design was being held in Monterey, California. One speaker demonstrated a compact disk, another an e-book and 3D graphics. There was a presentation on how to use fractal geometry to map coastlines. Four decades later, you need to be invited to this gathering. It is called the Annual Ted Conference and costs 10,000 dollars to attend.

What did a journalist, born in a remote village in Pakistan, have to do with this?

Chris Anderson believes that there is much to be gained by listening to people with different perspectives and backgrounds. Chris's father was an eye surgeon who ran medical camps in rural India, Pakistan, and Afghanistan. Till the eighth grade, Chris attended Woodstock School in Mussoorie and later studied in England. Chris loved cricket and cheered for Indian cricketers, including the Nawab of Pataudi and B.S. Chandrasekhar, who were touring England at the time.

After studying philosophy, politics, and economics at Oxford, Chris worked as a journalist in Seychelles. He later started a publishing house in England. Initially focussed on computers, Chris expanded the portfolio to include cycling, music, and design.

Visiting a TED conference, Chris was intrigued by the diverse background of the speakers and the conversations among the 'dreamers and optimists' present there. In 2001, his non-profit Sapling Foundation acquired TED. In quick succession, Chris introduced initiatives like TED Global, the TED prize, and audio and video podcasts. TEDx was also launched to host independently organized regional events.

Grounded in the principle of 'radical openness', TED is popular for the quality of its speakers and ideas that inspire change. Many videos have been viewed over a billion times on various platforms. TED Talks can be eclectic, with topics ranging from how wasps turn cockroaches into zombie guards to how chimpanzees differ from humans.

Ken Robinson is an author, speaker, and expert on education. In the widely viewed TED Talk 'Do Schools Kill Creativity?', he cautions against boxing young minds into compartments. Ideas should flow across disciplines and silos:

> *We think visually, we think in sound, we think*
> *kinaesthetically . . . we think in abstract terms, we*
> *think in movement . . . more often than not [original*
> *ideas] come about through the interaction of different*
> *disciplinary ways of seeing things.*

This integration of disciplines, geographies, and contexts can lead to unexpected outcomes. Remember Manjul enjoyed solving complex maths problems while listening to music and playing with toys.

Matt Ridley, a journalist and businessman, asserts that from as early as the Pleistocene period,[*] the meeting and mating of ideas have enabled human evolution:

> *You need to understand how human beings bring*
> *together their brains and enable their ideas to combine*
> *and recombine to meet and indeed to mate. In other*
> *words, you have to understand how ideas have sex.*

When ideas mate, they are drawing on a lineage of multiple clans rather than their own family. Let us see this in the way fishing tools and tackles have evolved over time.

Foraging tools were used by Oceanic Islanders in the South Pacific. Researchers have found that regions with smaller populations had less complex and diverse fishing tools. For instance, Hawaii with a population of 275,000 had seven times the number of fishing tools as Malekula, an island of 1,100 people. The tools used by the Hawaiians were also twice

---

[*] Often referred to as the Ice Age, it lasted from 2.5 million years to 11,700 years ago.

as complex. In other words, larger populations, with more collective minds, inspired new ideas that led to better tools.

When controlled for population size,* the complexity and variety of tools also depended on how remote an island was. Islands near each other were likely to trade and explore beyond their shores. Exchanging ideas with fellow traders led to better tools being developed.

Ridley uses the analogy of a room in which multiple conversations are taking place. When people converse in that room, it is not important how clever they are, but how many other rooms they are in contact with. The Internet is a modern-day tool where ideas multiply and grow. Think of an idea originating in Bengaluru, mating with one from Boston, and then recombining with another from Beijing. This can result in unexpected outcomes and even entrepreneurial opportunities as we will see later in this book.

TED speakers are just one of the modern-day evangelists promoting the combining and recombining of ideas. Awareness of the power and knowledge that can result when ideas mate has been with us for a long time.

The Renaissance,† with its sociocultural transitions, is often compared to removing a veil around a person's eyes to allow clear and unhindered vision. In *The Medici Effect: Breakthrough Insights at the Intersection of Ideas, Concepts, and Cultures*, Frans Johansson describes how innovation happens when disciplines combine and ideas intersect with each other. Florence's economy attracted sculptors, scientists, poets, and philosophers. The intersection of fields and disciplines paved the way for new

---

* Keeping population constant and removing its influence from the data set being analysed.
† Period of transition from the Middles Ages to modernity around the 15th and 16th centuries in European history.

concepts and existing ones to be combined in different ways. Europe, in this era, became a hotbed for unconventional thinking.

Of Frogs and Birds

While describing his field, Freeman Dyson, the theoretical and mathematical physicist, uses a metaphor of frogs and birds. Frogs, who live in the mud, can only see flowers growing nearby. They notice details and understand deep aspects of a problem that they engage with. Birds, on the other hand, fly high and view a wider and more varied landscape. This helps them make diverse and interesting connections that the frogs miss.

Are you a frog or a bird?

To thrive, you need to be both. Building a T-shaped profile, exploring a liberal education, and acting as a deliberate amateur are three pillars of dancing with disciplines.

DANCE WITH DISCIPLINES

build a
T-SHAPED
PROFILE

explore a
LIBERAL
EDUCATION

act as a
DELIBERATE
AMATEUR

Build a T-Shaped Profile

In our class on Design Thinking, we ask our students:

How can we tackle a wicked problem?

This leaves many of them puzzled, wondering what makes a problem wicked. It is a problem with interdependencies, one that has changing requirements and may even be difficult to define. An attempt to solve one aspect of a wicked problem could even complicate the original problem.

We encourage students to think about wicked problems like climate change, poverty, global hunger, and terrorism. To this list we now add the pandemic and discuss its challenges. Many countries initially enforced nationwide lockdowns leading to severe economic consequences. Clearly, the response to the pandemic has to account for people's lives and livelihoods.

There are wicked problems at the workplace as well. Traditional tools and techniques, no matter how sophisticated, may not be of much help in solving them.

During the class discussion, we pull this slide up.

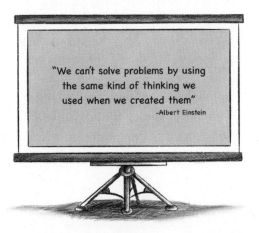

To solve wicked problems, you need to think differently. How can you do that?

One way is to look beyond your knowledge and expertise. For that you need to build a T-shaped profile. The letter 'T' has two parts, a vertical and a horizontal one. The vertical represents depth of knowledge in a particular field while the horizontal is about being a generalist. T-shaped people are experts in their own fields with a broad knowledge of others. This enables them to collaborate and engage with diverse disciplines.

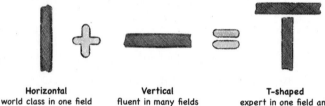

Horizontal
world class in one field

Vertical
fluent in many fields

T-shaped
expert in one field and
collaborative across others

In Chapter 3, we learned how Google looks for T-shaped employees. IDEO, a design and consulting firm, has people from various backgrounds working together. David Kelly, IDEO's founder, imagines a fleet of boats anchored together. A boat sometimes leaves to explore new areas, eventually returning to its moorings with new skills and competencies to share:

> *The best leaders will integrate emerging new disciplines quite skilfully, for example, [by bringing] in a food scientist to work alongside an industrial designer . . . the most interesting things always happen.*

In a deep dive, IDEO took on a project to redesign a shopping cart. ABC's *Nightline* featured them doing this in just five days. Multidisciplinary teams worked together on the challenge. While each team built its own prototype, the final cart had the best features of each model. There were hooks to hang shopping bags, open baskets, wheels with a quick turning radius, an automated checkout system, and child safety features. Some of the mantras IDEO adopts for innovation include flattening hierarchies, deferring judgement, building on the ideas of others, and accepting that chaos can be constructive.

When David was a student at Stanford University, design as a discipline nestled between two domains: art and engineering. Art focussed on aesthetics and ergonomics while engineering embraced technology. At IDEO, design is a mindset, an approach that focusses on the verb rather than the noun.

Tom Peters, a business writer, describes IDEO as a zoo:

> *Experts of all flavours co-mingle in offices that look more like cacophonous kindergarten classrooms. Walk into the offices of IDEO in Palo Alto, California, immediately you'll be caught up in the energy, buzz, creative disarray, and sheer lunacy of it all.*

Explore a Liberal Education

> *A liberal education does not teach you how to make a living but rather how to make a life.*
>
> —Fareed Zakaria

Yale University is known for its liberal arts curriculum, where students are trained to be deep generalists. They acquire depth through a major and breadth through study areas (arts, humanities, sciences, social sciences) and skill areas (writing, quantitative reasoning, foreign languages). During the initial two years, students study a variety of courses and are exposed to diverse intellectual philosophies. They then immerse themselves in a fundamental discipline while being exposed to many others. This enables them to think across disciplines and even use one as a lens to examine another.

Unfortunately, a liberal education is often confused with liberal arts. 'Liberal' is even misused to imply class privilege. The word liberal is derived from the Latin word *liber*, which means free. Ancient Greeks and Romans considered a liberal education essential for people to be free and liberated from the confines of their family profession.

A liberal approach can be used to understand and learn any subject. To be a historian, students don't just study history; they study the trivium comprising grammar, rhetoric and dialectic. This is followed by the quadrivium of geometry, arithmetic, music and astronomy.

Critical thinking allows us to think rationally, visualize connections across disciplines, and form a perspective. 'The Future of Jobs', a report by the World Economic Forum, lists critical thinking as among the top three skills required to navigate the new landscape. This report, published in the pre-pandemic era, is even more relevant today.

Liberal education fellowships and degree programmes are becoming popular in India. The Naropa Fellowship, where we have taught, has a one-year residential postgraduate programme tailored for the Himalayan region. Currently located near the

Shey monastery in Ladakh, it is set to move to its new campus in Hemis, about 30 kilometres southeast of Leh.

The fellowship was started by Pramath Sinha, who also co-founded Ashoka University. Students spend a year living in Leh's sub-zero winters with patchy Internet and intermittent water supply.

What do they gain from this?

Pramath explains:

> *It is the way you are taught, not just what you are taught. Remember some of the problems you will confront don't even have an answer . . . the ability to think for yourself even if you are not taught something, that's the benefit of a liberal education.*

* * *

Students often ask us if they should opt for skill-based courses or pursue their interests. Many have heard the story of Steve Jobs, who was a liberal arts student before he dropped out of college. Years later he recalled the calligraphy class he had sat in on:

> *I learned about serifs and sans-serif typefaces, about varying the space between different letter combinations, about what makes great typography great. It was beautiful. Historical. Artistically subtle in a way that science cannot capture.*

The class was taught by Robert Palladino. At 17, Robert had joined the Trappist Order and lived a monastic life for two decades. His elegant writing caught the attention of the monastery scribe. One day, the creator of Reed College's calligraphy programme invited the artist to study in his advanced-level class.

Soon Robert renounced his monastic lifestyle and joined Reed College eventually heading its calligraphy department. Robert had an unusual teaching style, emphasizing silence and the need to take a step back and observe carefully. His elective course attracted students from many disciplines. Fine design emerged from conversations around philosophy, history, literature, and religious thought.

Steve often said that you can only connect the dots in hindsight. Years after they graduate, some of our students too share similar experiences. They find the exposure they have had to multiple disciplines encourages them to think critically about problems at work.

Do employers value a liberal education?

In the American comedy-drama film *Liberal Arts*, 35-year-old Jesse, played by Josh Radnor, returns to his college campus. There he meets Zibby, played by Elizabeth Olsen, who is much younger than him. In one scene, Zibby asks Jesse about his major in college:

> *I was English [sic] with a minor in history. Just to make sure I was fully unemployable.*

Jesse's answer raises a question many students (and their parents) often ask us. In an age of computers and artificial intelligence, do companies need liberal arts graduates?

Yes, they do, says Tom Perreault.

Tom was the Chief People Officer of Rally Health, a digital health company. He feels philosophy and history majors have the leadership skills that will make them the CEOs of tomorrow:

> *What can't be replaced in any organization imaginable in the future are the liberal arts skills, such as creativity, empathy, listening, and vision. These skills, not digital or technological ones, will hold the keys to a company's future success.*

* * *

What if, like us, you too have had a traditional education and specialized in one primary discipline?

Here are two paths before you.

First, spend time with people from backgrounds dissimilar to yours. Our classes in entrepreneurship have students majoring in philosophy, computer science, economics, and literature all coming together to analyse a business case. Each student views the challenges the case throws up from a different perspective. This leads to a rich class discussion where students, as well as faculty, learn from each other. Hence, the dedication in this book is *to our students, who teach us every day.*

Second, just being aware of the power of a multidisciplinary approach will encourage you to explore subjects outside your domain. This is like adopting a growth mindset simply by being aware of its value, which we encountered in Chapter 3. As early and mid-career professionals, you can also gain the benefits of a liberal education by doing hybrid and online courses.

Act as a Deliberate Amateur

Children are curious. They question everything and ask:

- Why?
- Why not?
- How?
- When?

And finally: How do you know?

Children are trying to make sense of the world around them. We adults often run out of patience and remind them *curiosity killed the cat.*

Curiosity, in fact, helps children think critically and can even influence their academic performance. Some studies indicate that curiosity may be as important as intelligence in predicting how well students do in school.

A desire for knowledge can motivate adults to examine new ideas. Curiosity will lead you into fields you are unfamiliar with. You will eventually become better at learning and connecting unrelated information and solving problems that are novel and complex.

How can adults learn to be curious?

Andre, the physicist who made a frog levitate, believes in engaging with new fields and challenging their paradigms:

> *We are entering into someone else's territory, to be frank, and questioning things people who work in that area never bother to ask.*

Andre is a deliberate amateur.

The word amateur is from the Latin word *amator* meaning lover, paramour, or admirer. It was meant to describe a person who indulges in an activity for pleasure. Unfortunately, it is often used to imply a lack of knowledge and experience.

Deliberate amateurs resist being socialized. Most people tend to internalize the norms, beliefs and values of the field they are in. Edward de Bono, author of *Six Thinking Hats*, was a physician and psychologist as well as a philosopher and inventor. An advocate of *lateral thinking*, he wanted 'thinking' to be taught as a subject in schools and warned of the dangers of familiarity:

> *Too much experience within a field may restrict creativity because you know so well how things should be done that you are unable to escape and have new ideas.*

Deliberate amateurs, like Andre, avoid being socialized by their profession. They explore disciplines that interest them without worrying how they are connected. Saikat Majumdar, our colleague at Ashoka University, feels that being torn between disciplines is a sign of intellectual curiosity. When undecided about choosing between two majors, say, physics and philosophy or maths and music, students should study both.

This was the way Manjul chose his courses at university. Majoring in mathematics, he also studied music and Sanskrit. Ultimately, this approach encourages students to view one discipline through the lens of another while making connections across seemingly unrelated fields. Saikat calls this a *contra-disciplinary approach*.

What happens if two disciplines, particularly those with different philosophies and research methodologies, collide? Rather than a roadblock, this can throw up opportunities to develop new insights and ways of thinking.

Ashish Dhawan, founder and trustee at Ashoka University, feels that this approach ensures that even traditional fields offer new value propositions. He gives the example of computer science:

> *The future of computer science is the intersection between that [computer science] and other disciplines like computational biology, computational astrophysics or even digital humanities.*

At first glance, digital humanities may sound like an oxymoron. The field is so new that it is yet to even have a universally accepted definition. It broadly covers the intersection of digital technologies and humanities. This provides an opportunity for researchers to use digital tools and technology to analyse large volumes of literary data.

Sentiment analysis, for example, enables researchers to find out how people feel about a topic or even a word or phrase. Imagine tweeting about a Bollywood political thriller. Your tweet, and those of others, is now part of a larger data set. By collating them, experts can assess how audiences feel about the movie, whether opinions vary across geographic areas, and if there is an age or gender divide in perceptions.

Are people cheering for your Indian Premier League (IPL) cricket team? What do 100 books you have not yet read reveal about a topic you are interested in? How do young people feel about climate change?

The mating of two fields can also alter their boundaries. Technology has enabled researchers in the humanities to ask questions they could not have engaged with earlier. Similarly, humanistic enquiry is now possible about the way technology is impacting our lives.

So What?

It is the morning of 13 January 1942.

You wake up to the sound of bombing in wartime London. Picking up *The Daily Telegraph* you notice a prize of 100 pounds for solving the day's crossword puzzle.

Take a few minutes to solve it. In fact, you have 12 minutes.

If you succeed, an envelope marked 'confidential' will arrive in your mail. You will be requested to meet Colonel Nichols of the General Staff, who 'would very much like to see you on a matter of national importance'. After receiving security clearance, you will have to sign the Official Secrets Act.

You are now an employee of the British Secret Intelligence Service and work at Bletchley Park, about 50 miles north of London. Inside this Victorian country estate are wooden huts, each designated with only a number.

Your instructions are:

> *Do no talk at meals. Do not talk in the transport. Do not talk while travelling. Do not talk in the billet. Do not talk by your own fireside. Be careful even in your hut.*

Telegraph Crossword 5,062   Unknown

ACROSS

1. A stage company (6)
4. The direct route preferred by the Roundhead (5, 3)
9. One of the evergreens (6)
10. Scented (8)
12. Course with an apt finish (5)
13. Much that could be got from a timber merchant (5, 4)
15. We have nothing and are in debt (3)
16. Pretend (5)
17. Is this town ready for a flood? (6)
22. The little fellow has some beer; it makes me lose colour, I say (6)
24. Fashion of a famous French family (5)
27. Tree (3)
28. One might of course use this tool to core an apple (6, 3)
31. Once used for unofficial currency (5)
32. Those well brought up help these over styles (4, 4)
33. A sport in a hurry (6)
34. Is the workshop that turns out this part of a motor a hush hush affair (8)
35. An illumination functioning (6)

DOWN

1. Official instruction not to forget the servants (8)
2. Said to be a remedy for a burn (5, 3)
3. Kind of alias (9)
5. A disagreeable company (5)
6. Debtors may have to this money for their debts unless of course their creditors do it to the debts (5)
7. Boat that should be able to suit anyone (6)
8. Gear (6)
11. Business with an end in sight (6)
14. The right sort of woman to start a dame school (3)
18. "The war" (anag) (6)
19. When hammering take care not to hit this (5, 4)
20. Making sound as a bell (8)
21. Half a fortnight of old (8)
23. Bird, dish or coin (3)
25. This sign of the zodiac has no connection with the fishes (6)
26. A preservative of teeth (6)
29. Famous sculptor (5)
30. This part of a locomotive engine would sound familiar to a golfer (5)

© 13 January 1942

These were dangerous times. Germany had carpet-bombed London and appeared to be winning the war. The US had sent convoys of merchant ships across the Atlantic with food, oil, and other essential supplies. Many of these ships were torpedoed; others were sitting ducks for the German U-boats hunting them. Allied leadership was worried that Britain could be on its way to starvation.

German headquarters communicated with their U-boats using code generated from a cipher device* called *Enigma*. It resembled a small typewriter with an electromechanical rotor that scrambled the letters of the alphabet. The rotor settings were changed every day. Recipients of the messages had a list of codes and would decrypt incoming communication using the same settings as the transmitting station. Enigma could generate 60 septillion† combinations.

Codebreakers at Bletchley Park were trying to decipher the code and anticipate German movement. Bletchley Park was chosen as it was easily accessible from both Oxford and Cambridge, the universities that were expected to be the main hiring ground for codebreakers.

British military intelligence needed unconventional thinkers. The team at Bletchley Park had mathematicians, cryptographers, historians, and chess champions. They even recruited a papyrology specialist who had spent years studying ancient literature and legal archives. The team was headed by Alan Turing, a mathematician and computer scientist.

Once the team working at Bletchley Park automated the search for the right settings, they were able to decode messages and identify the location of the U-boats. American ships then changed course to avoid the German 'wolf packs', and the Allies began targeting Germany's naval assets. By the summer of 1943, acting on messages they had intercepted, Allied forces had sunk over 70 German submarines.

Historians believe codebreakers at Bletchley Park shortened the war by at least two years and saved more than 14 million

---

* Ciphers are algorithms for encrypting and decrypting data.
† A septillion is a 1000 raised to the 8th power.

lives. Winston Churchill, Britain's prime minister during the war, admitted that his biggest fear had been the peril of German U-boats. He described the Bletchley Park codebreakers as 'the geese that laid the golden eggs but never cackled'.

Much of Turing's work went unrecognized in his lifetime. In 1952, he was convicted of homosexuality and accepted chemical castration to avoid a prison sentence. Turing later committed suicide. His life has been poignantly captured in the award-winning film, *The Imitation Game*.

Turing was posthumously pardoned by Queen Elizabeth II and his life celebrated with a royal stamp. The Turing Award, named after him, is considered the most prestigious recognition in computer science and the equivalent of the Nobel Prize.

From Andre Giem the physicist to Allan Turing the codebreaker, we have seen how dancing with disciplines can lead to new opportunities and ways of thinking.

Are you adventurous enough to dance with them?

A human being should be able to change a diaper,
plan an invasion, butcher a hog, conn a ship,
design a building, write a sonnet, balance accounts,
build a wall, set a bone, comfort the dying,
take orders, give orders, cooperate, act alone,
solve equations, analyze a new problem,
pitch manure, program a computer,
cook a tasty meal, fight efficiently,
die gallantly.
Specialization is for insects.
—Robert Heinlein (1907–1988),
American science fiction writer

5

CURATE THE CHAOS

cutting the clutter

> *The fact that you are still working for me, tells me I'm not doing my job. You should be out, going after more of your goals and dreams.*

Warren Buffet is talking to Mike Flint, his personal pilot of several years.

Warren has a 5/25 rule:

Step 1: Write down your top 25 goals.
Step 2: Draw a circle around your top 5.
Step 3: Focus on them.

Mike wrote down his goals and circled five of them:

> **Warren:** *What about the ones you didn't circle?*

> **Mike:** *The top five are my primary focus, but the other 20 come in a close second. They are still important so I will work on those intermittently. They are not urgent, but I still plan to give them a dedicated effort.*

> **Warren:** *No, you've got it wrong Mike. Everything you didn't circle just became an avoid-at-all-costs list. No matter what these things, they get no attention from you until you have succeeded with your top five.*

This was advice on how to choose your personal goals and work towards them. Here is another story, this time about making choices for others.

Tumaini Basaninyenzi (Tuma) was born in Congo and moved to the US when he was five years old. After graduating from the University of Iowa, he did an MBA at the Stern School at New York University. On a visit to Africa, Tuma discovered hip-hop. He then spent a decade working at MTV before joining Spotify as the Global Programme Head of Hip-Hop.

Tuma's playlist, 'RapCaviar', has 14 million followers:

> *I am not a creator; I am a curator. So the music has to be right. For me to authorise a song, the song has to be real. Realness in terms of this is what people like; that this came from the heart.*

Tuma discovers, organizes, and disseminates music. He is a gatekeeper between record labels and listeners. For Tuma curation involves exploring and selecting a combination that tells a new story.

This chapter is about cutting the clutter around us. It is about narrowing your choices with simple rules. You can then focus on the essential by detecting and later debunking bullshit.

Economists tell us that the more choices we have, the happier we should be. In a jam experiment, shoppers had a choice to buy from 6 or 24 varieties of jam. Which option do you think were they happier with?

Like Warren Buffet's advice to his pilot, Marie Kondo also focusses on the essential. Her book on ways to declutter your home is a *New York Times* bestseller. *Tidying up with Marie Kondo*, her Netflix series, has been renewed for a second season.

We will later peep into a class at the University of Washington. The course is about learning to call out bullshit. In the first class, students reflect on the bullshit surrounding them, the extent to which they contribute to it, and how they can debunk it. The course gets filled up as soon as registration opens.

At the end of this chapter, we will meet Maria Popova, a Bulgarian-American writer and curator, who shares material on art, philosophy, and culture. Maria is a curator who would like to leave you with *a thought, an idea, a question.*

The Foreign and the Familiar

Many people believe that curation is the act of selecting and presenting content. Some view it as cross-pollinating ideas to make a meaningful collection. Others think of curation as a way to learn and grow.

It is, in fact, a mix of all of these.

Curation brings together the foreign and the familiar. We listen to songs we like while looking for new music that is foreign yet familiar in certain ways.

Rohit Bhargava, an adjunct professor at Georgetown University, publishes the Non-Obvious series of books. In 2009, Rohit predicted that there would be a new category of people working online. He called them 'content curators'.

Manifesto-Job Description

In the near-future experts predict content on the web will double every 72 hours. The detached analysis of an algorithm will no longer be enough to find out what we are looking for. To satisfy the people's hunger for great content on any topic imaginable, there will need to be a new category of individuals working online. Someone whose job is not to create more content but to make sense of all the content that others are creating.
To find the best and most relevant content and bring it forward. The people who chose to take on this role will be known as

Content Curators

Is Rohit's idea of finding the best, most relevant content and presenting it a new one?

Let's travel back a hundred years.

As a 25-year-old, DeWitt Wallace enlisted in the US Army and served in World War I. Injured in battle, he spent several months recuperating in a hospital in France. Flipping through magazines, DeWitt was struck by the sheer amount of content available and the difficulty in reading it all.

Back home, DeWitt began visiting the public library in Minneapolis. He catalogued articles and condensed them into a format that was easy to read. A friend's sister, Lila Acheson, liked the idea. Putting together 31 articles from well-known magazines, DeWitt sent them to publishers. Some articles were abridged versions of the originals that had been shortened while still retaining the authors' style and storyline. All publishers turned him down.

DeWitt and Lila were now married. Before leaving on their honeymoon, they mailed several hundred flyers advertising a 'magazine of magazines'. The couple returned to find that 133 subscribers had paid three dollars each for an annual subscription to their compilation. They called it *Reader's Digest*.

Initially published from the basement of their home, *Reader's Digest* is the largest paid circulation magazine in the world. It compiles articles on a range of topics from health to home décor and politics to real-life stories. Some articles continue to be rewritten or are translations from other languages. Each edition has a long-form story that has been extracted and condensed from a book.

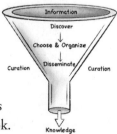

The hallmark of *Reader's Digest* is curation. It involves discovering, organizing, and disseminating content. Imagine a funnel that receives information at one end and churns out distilled knowledge at the other.

Curation adds value to content that may have otherwise gone unnoticed. In a way curation is also creation; it results in a new genre that attracts and retains the interest of users who consume and share it.

You are a curator when you process information, weigh alternatives, and make decisions. How can you become a better curator?

The practice of curation stands on three pillars: narrow your choices with simple rules, focus on the essential, and detect and debunk bullshit.

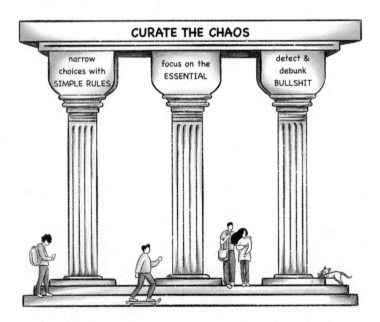

Narrow Your Choices with Simple Rules

Can less be more?

Marketing experts contend that we are all rational decision-makers and have well-ordered preferences. Hence, more choices will make us happier.

Sheena Iyengar, a professor of business at Columbia Business School, is the author of *The Art of Choosing*. Her research looks at factors that influence choices and the way we can improve our decision-making.

Sheena's own choices were initially shaped by her circumstances:

> *I was three when I was diagnosed with retinitis pigmentosa and by then I was legally blind, so it was clear, early on, that choices were being taken away.*

Sheena's father, a Sikh immigrant, passed away when she was 13. Her mother wanted her to be independent and self-reliant. In 1997, Sheena earned a PhD in social psychology from Stanford University.

While a student, Sheena often visited Draeger's, a supermarket in Menlo Park, California. Draeger's is not a regular grocery store; it is known for stocking a large variety of products. Customers can choose from 250 varieties of mustard, 75 types of olive oil, and 300 flavours of jam. While Sheena enjoyed visiting Draeger's, she often returned empty-handed.

Was Sheena overwhelmed by the variety of choices she had to select from?

To find out, Sheena and a colleague tried an experiment. On two consecutive Sundays, they set up a tasting booth at the entrance of the store. The booth offered either 6 varieties of jam (limited choice) or 24 varieties (extended choice). The set-up was rotated every hour. Two research assistants stood by and invited shoppers to sample the jams. An observer recorded the number of people who stopped by the booth and those who walked past it.

Which booth do you think attracted more shoppers?

Among those who walked by the extended choice booth, 60 per cent stopped to sample the jam. The number for the limited choice booth was 40 per cent.

So, you are better off with more choices.

Not quite.

The more relevant question is: *which booth sold more jam?*

Visitors to the booth got a discount coupon to purchase any flavour of jam they liked from the store. Jams were stacked on racks behind the tasting booths. Among those who stopped by the limited choice booth, 30 per cent made a purchase. At the extended choice booth only 3 per cent bought jam.

People who bought

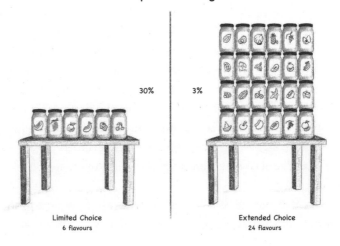

30% 3%

Limited Choice
6 flavours

Extended Choice
24 flavours

As part of the study, observers hid behind the racks to observe shoppers' behaviour. They found that shoppers coming from the booth with extended choice appeared puzzled and even confused. Some looked around for a while and left without buying. In contrast, shoppers from the booth with limited choice walked confidently to the rack, made a selection, and left.

This experiment challenges conventional thinking that the more choices we have, the better off we are. In fact, with fewer choices, we may find it easier to decide and are less likely to procrastinate. After the purchase, we are also happier and more satisfied than if we had many choices. The act of choosing can sometimes be difficult and even intimidating.

Even while making a simple decision, we tend to examine the options carefully when there are many choices available. This requires greater decision-making effort. We may then decide not to take any decision at all. Decisions can be easier when we have limited options.

How can we narrow our choices?

Follow simple rules.

For managers, simple rules bridge the gap between strategy and execution and provide flexibility while making decisions. This allows managers freedom to exercise their judgement and makes the act of choosing easier.

Can simple rules help run a café, frame better human resource policies, play poker professionally and even eat well? These examples will show you how effective simple rules can be.

The youngest in his class, Sanjiv Suri was proud that he could learn and perform like everyone else. At 24, after working as a chef, he went to France and pursued a master's degree in hospitality.

Sanjiv got a job as the general manager of a hotel in Liberia. There, he met his Swedish girlfriend, with whom he later moved to Prague. After spending three years travelling across Europe, Sanjiv set up a small café under the stairway of the National Museum in Prague.

Today Sanjiv owns the Zátiší Group, a fine dining and catering business in downtown Prague that runs 3 of the top 10 restaurants in the city. Besides event catering, the group has a 'Fresh and Tasty' division, which provides healthy meals to corporates and school canteens.

Sanjiv faced several bottlenecks in growing his business. The chefs, many of whom had been with him for years, enjoyed complete autonomy in picking their menus. Hence, the group could not avail of discounts or make bulk purchases. The chefs valued novelty and cooked nearly 1,000 different recipes. Even bestselling dishes were rarely repeated. Due to their originality and variety, many dishes required ingredients that were not fresh or even locally available.

In *Simple Rules*, Donald Sull and Kathleen Eisenhardt describe how Sanjiv de-bottlenecked his business. Going forward, all chefs would finalize the following week's menu by Wednesday afternoon.

Menus would be drawn up using simple rules:

- At least three out of the five dishes are bestsellers from the past.
- At least two dishes are common across all cafeterias.
- 90 per cent of the produce is seasonal or locally sourced.

After implementing these simple rules, revenues shot up and profits doubled.

* * *

Can simple rules help frame better human resource policies?

Netflix realized that using logic and common sense, 97 per cent of their employees would make the right choices at work. Was it worth writing, monitoring and enforcing detailed policy documents for the remaining 3 per cent?

Till 2012, Patty McCord was the chief talent officer at Netflix. In a *Harvard Business Review* article, she wrote:

> *Trust people, not policies.*
> *Reward candour.*
> *And throw away the standard playbook.*

Netflix's expense policy is 'Act in Netflix's best interests'. Employees should:

- expend only what you would otherwise not spend,
- travel as you would if it were your own money,
- disclose non-trivial gifts from vendors, and
- take from Netflix only when it is inefficient not to take and inconsequential.

In 2009, Netflix shared its culture deck on the web. Over the next five years, it was viewed five million times. Sheryl Sandberg, then COO of Metaverse, calls it 'the most important document to have emerged from Silicon Valley'. It reflects the company's objectives of hiring the best talent. In case there is a mistake, or if the employee's skills no longer fit the organization, Reed Hastings, CEO of Netflix, believes in letting them go:

> *[Just] adequate performance gets a generous severance package.*

Strategic fit is a management concept in which various activities in an organization are aligned and reinforce each other. Netflix's essential goal is to enhance employee performance. Realizing that most employees will do the right thing, Netflix uses simple rules to shape the company's culture. This allows employees to focus on strategic processes that enhance their, and the organization's, value.

* * *

Now let's see how simple rules helped a graduate student learn to play poker professionally. Raghu Shukla grew up in Chennai, attended the Delhi University, and then studied mathematics in the US. Later, while a graduate student of computer science at Stanford University, Raghu was drawn to poker.

Raghu initially took an online course and read several books on the game. Playing with friends at a local casino, he gradually increased his stakes from a dollar to 5 and 10 dollars. One day, Raghu lost heavily to a player who played poorly but was lucky. Raghu was forced to manage his finances by eating only cereal until his next graduate student paycheck arrived.

Re-examining his approach to poker, Raghu set simple rules for himself:

- Never play for amounts you can't afford to lose.
- Don't play emotionally.
- Mix strategies when in the company of sharks and fish.

The first two rules are evident. Raghu explains the third one:

> *Las Vegas poker is a game of sharks and fish. If you*
> *are the shark, you win. But if you look around the*

table and see only sharks, then you're probably the
fish, and it's time to leave.

* * *

Finally, can you maintain healthy eating habits by following simple rules?

Michael Pollan is an author, journalist, and professor—the order in which he describes himself. Best known for his books on food and its social and cultural impact, Michael's advice for a healthy and sustainable diet is to avoid products containing ingredients that:

- are unfamiliar,
- are unpronounceable,
- are more than five in number, and
- contain high fructose corn syrup.

To eat wisely follow three rules:

i) *eat food,*
ii) *mostly plants,*
iii) *not too much.*

What we eat today is often not food. It is merely something that appeals to our sense of taste. Michael says we should only eat what our great-grandmother would recognize as food. In support of eating mostly plants, he quotes medical research on the value of a fruit and plant-based diet.

Other studies uphold Michael's third rule: not too much. Dan Buettner has examined the role that regions and cultures play in shaping healthier and longer lives. In Okinawa, an island at the southern tip of Japan, before eating, elders repeat the Confucian proverb 'hara hachi bu'.

It means eat till you are 80 per cent full.

Focus on the Essential

Marie Kondo is so well known in Japan that she no longer rides the Tokyo metro. Soft-spoken and petite, Marie is a professional organizer who helps people declutter their homes.

As a child after returning from school, Marie could barely wait to put her bag down before she began to find things to throw away. Her parents tolerated this for a while, eventually forbidding Marie from tidying up their home.

Marie celebrated her 18th birthday with a visit to Japan's National Library. One of the largest in the world, it only permits adults to enter. Marie spent her birthday browsing through books on tidying, decluttering, and organizing.

In Japan, the zeal for being organized has cultural roots. Living spaces are small, and with rising consumerism, keeping homes uncluttered can be a challenge. In Shintoism,* tidying and cleaning are considered forms of mental cultivation and spiritual training.

While tidying up the homes of her friends, Marie realized this could become her profession. Over the years, she has written several books on it and has a Netflix show that helps people clear junk from their homes.

---

* A belief system that originated in Japan and is followed by many people worldwide.

The 'KonMarie Method' of decluttering has spawned an industry in the US, where even people with large suburban homes reach out for help. Marie's first book, *The Life Changing Magic of Tidying Up*, has sold over eight million copies and has been translated into many languages.

It did not begin that way.

In 2010, Marie submitted a book proposal to a training programme called 'How to write bestsellers that will be loved for ten years'. She won the first prize. One judge, who was the editor and publisher of self-help books, felt the proposal had promise. Over a period of eight months, he mentored Marie and helped her write the book. After it was published, he made Marie tidy the house of a well-known comedian. Stories of that experience were then uploaded on the Internet. Gradually, book sales began to pick up.

Later that year, the Tohuku earthquake and tsunami hit Japan. Nearly 20,000 people lost their lives and many more their possessions.* This made people introspect and question what was important to them. Many Japanese went back to their roots and began to adopt a simpler lifestyle.

Marie's Netflix show, *Tidying Up with Marie Kondo*, has been renewed for a second season. Like Google and Uber, Marie's name has become a verb. Don't be surprised to hear, 'I am Kondoing my closet' or even 'She finally Kondo'd the guy she was dating'.

While decluttering your home or workplace, you tend to select items you don't need and throw them away. It's intuitive to discard non-essential things.

---

* The Tohuku earthquake and the following tsunami are often referred to as the Great East Japan earthquake or simply as 3.11 for the date they occurred on.

Marie soon learnt otherwise:

> *I realized my mistake: I was only looking for things to throw out. What I should be doing is finding the things I want to keep. Identifying the things that make you happy: that is the work of tidying.*

* * *

Like Marie, Japan has another icon who, for over eight decades, has focussed on doing what is essential. This story is about sushi and, more importantly, the 'shokunin'' behind it.

How much would you be willing to pay to eat 20 pieces of sushi in a restaurant located in the basement of a subway station in Tokyo?

It will cost you 30,000 yen (about 250 dollars) and take about 20 minutes to eat.

Sukiyabashi Jiro was the first sushi restaurant to be awarded three Michelin stars. *Eater Magazine*, published by Vox Media, ranked it among the 11 toughest restaurants in the world to get a reservation.

As a nine-year-old, Jiro Ono ran away from home. He has been making sushi ever since. Chefs in his restaurant train for 10 years before being allowed to cut fish or cook it. The hot towel you get before beginning your meal has been hand-squeezed by an apprentice who is training to become a chef.

Jiro has a network of vendors who have worked with him for decades and are entirely focussed on their craft. This includes suppliers of rice and vinegar, as well as seaweed and eel from the

---

* A Japanese word meaning mastery of one's profession.

local market. Jiro knows that the temperature of the cook's hand can alter the flavour of the fish. Before being cooked, an octopus is hand-massaged for 45 minutes to ensure that it has the right texture and taste.

All this has been captured by David Gelb in *Jiro Dreams of Sushi*. Our students watch this documentary in an introductory course on entrepreneurship. Its vivid cinematography celebrates Jiro's life. As vegetarians, though, we often hurry through the elaborate scenes of seafood being prepared.

Jiro is a shokunin. At 96, he remains dedicated to his craft and is still perfecting it. David, who once wanted to be a sushi chef himself, has a wider message:

> *This movie is about sushi, but sushi is just the setting. Look at what you are doing. Is this what you love to do? If it is, do your absolute best at it. If you don't like what you are doing, change something. Find something that you can just focus on and continue to improve at that.*

* * *

In aviation, a focus on the essential can be critical for safety. Aware that distractions and interruptions to the crew account for many airline incidents,* the Federal Aviation Administration formulated a 'sterile cockpit rule'. While the aircraft is flying below 10,000 feet, pilots are forbidden from engaging in any conversation or activity unrelated to the immediate business of flying.

---

* Federal Aviation Administration defines an incident as any occurrence that affects safe operations.

This rule was enforced after an aircraft crashed short of the runway while attempting to land in dense fog at Charlotte Douglas International Airport. An investigation later found that the pilots were distracted by idle chatter and unaware of the aircraft's altitude.

Whether you are cleaning your closet, cooking sushi, or flying an aircraft, focus on doing the essential. For that, you need to first identify what is not essential and eliminate it.

Detect and Debunk Bullshit

Momentous Sprint at the 2156 Olympics?

This was the title of an article in the September 2004 issue of the journal *Nature*. An accompanying graph had the 100-metre Olympic sprint timings of male and female athletes for the past 100 years. When extrapolated, these two lines intersect around 2156.

Will female athletes at the 2156 Olympic Games run faster than male sprinters?

Vidya Rajan, a high school biology teacher in Texas, asked her students to comment on the article. They found that the research method was 'riddled with flaws':

> *It is not logical to say that the first 104 years will have data with exactly the same regression as the next 148 years.*

Another reader wrote a letter that an even more exciting race would come up in 2636. That year, sprint timings of less than zero seconds would be recorded. Tongue in cheek, he suggested that the intervening 600 years should be used to improve the teaching of basic statistics and plan for the challenges that timekeepers would face.

Carl Bergstrom and Jevin West, both professors at the University of Washington, teach a course titled 'Calling Bullshit: Data Reasoning in a Digital World'. Each module in the course explores a facet of bullshit and ways to debunk it. The professors begin the course by asking students if they are 'bullshit neutral'. Students create a 'bullshit inventory' on the bullshit they are exposed to, the bullshit they produce, and how much of it they debunk. If the bullshit that they discredit is equal to that which they produce, they are bullshit neutral.

Ashoka University too offers a similar course. In this class, students debate whether bullshit is restricted to politics and humanities or if the sciences are susceptible to it too.

In 2008, an article in the medical journal *Obesity* asked, 'Will All Americans Become Overweight or Obese?' Examining obesity rates in the US, researchers concluded that 86 per cent of the adult population will be overweight by 2030. If that were true, then based on extrapolating data, *all* adults will be overweight by 2048.

Jorden Elleberg, a researcher, questioned the study's findings. As with the Olympic sprint timing, the critical assumption was *if present trends continue*. Extrapolating current trends shows 109 per cent of Americans will be overweight or obese by 2060. We must realize that the graph of present trends will naturally bend and then flatten over time.

* * *

Can ice cream sales lead to higher homicide rates?

This question is often used in an introductory course in statistics to illustrate how incorrect interpretation of data can lead to strange conclusions.

Studies show that homicides increase during warm weather. This could be due to larger numbers of people being outdoors and likelihood of arguments and fights breaking out. In hot weather, ice cream sales also increase. However, ice cream sales are not responsible for homicides. *Correlation is not causation.* Just because two variables are related, it does not mean that one causes the other. Sophisticated data mining tools can trawl large amounts of data and generate spurious correlations that need further analysis.

During the pandemic an article in the journal *Frontiers in Nutrition* received attention. Among the many conclusions it reached, one stood out: drinking one to four glasses of red wine every week could reduce the risk of contracting Covid by 17 per cent. Drinking white wine and champagne was also beneficial, though not to the same extent as red wine. The study explained that high levels of polyphenols in red wine could be activating proteins that in turn prevent cell death.

Should we all begin drinking red wine?

Colin Angus, a senior research fellow at the Sheffield Alcohol Research Group in the UK refuted this conclusion. It was not wine that was beneficial, but the associated lifestyle of wine drinkers and their socio-economic background that was probably responsible for this:

> *All this study shows us is that the kind of people who drink wine are also the kinds of people who have lower Covid risks because of many other factors unrelated to their wine drinking.*

For some, cutting the clutter can also be an entrepreneurial opportunity. Shekhar Gupta, a news journalist, is a prominent figure in both print and television. More recently, he has founded 'The Print', a digital media company. Shekhar also hosts a popular channel called Cut the Clutter. True to its name, the channel curates news by cutting the clutter around it.

The challenge of 'separating the wheat from the chaff' is not unique to our times. In 1914, the philosopher John Alexander Smith was talking to students at Oxford University:

> *If you work hard and intelligently you should be able to detect when a man is talking rot, and that, in my view, is the main, if not the sole, purpose of education.*

The millennials have Dhruv Rathee, whose channel covers topics ranging from the environment to personal finance and from travel to politics:

> *I realized the need to present actual research in front of them [viewers] so that they understand the truth.*

So What?

Maria Popova's grandmother wished that she would do the sensible thing. Maria, however, had other plans.

As a child, she would weave dolls using red and white wool. In Bulgaria, these dolls are a symbol of peace and health. Like many youngsters at that time, Maria dreamt of escaping post-communist Eastern Europe. After graduating from the American College of Sofia in 2003, Maria went to the US to study communications at an Ivy League university.

Maria was in a class of 400 students. The professor, who didn't even know the students' names, often read from slides. Maria found TED Talks more stimulating and realized that if she wanted a real education, she would have to craft one herself.

Maria worked part-time at an advertising agency. At her office, some of her colleagues would circulate emails with clippings of work done by rival agencies. Maria felt that she could do a better job. She began emailing seven friends every week, sharing five things unrelated to advertising. This was the beginning of her blog *Brain Pickings*, which is now *The Marginalian*.

Maria blogged about topics that were 'timeless and timely' and viewed it as a place for personal exploration. Her friends began to forward her emails to their friends, with the blog becoming increasingly popular. Maria realized there was an intellectual yearning for the interdisciplinary perspective and self-learning she provided her readers.

After graduation, Maria received offers to work in marketing and business. She wondered if she should spend 80 per cent of her day at a job she did not enjoy and hope the money would make it bearable. Alternatively, she could pursue something she loved and let the money figure itself out.

Maria decided to learn web designing. Eating oatmeal and tuna for breakfast, lunch, and dinner, she saved to sign up for a night class. Due to visa regulations, Maria was forced to leave the US and return to Bulgaria. Maria eventually got a job in Los Angeles and later moved to New York. During these years, living in various apartments, continents and cities, Maria continued to nurture her website and post on it.

The Marginalian is now an online platform covering disciplines from design and science to philosophy and poetry. Maria describes herself as a 'Curiosity Sherpa':

There's information, which is just noise. There's knowledge, which is your understanding of that information. And then there's wisdom, which is your ability to apply that knowledge to how you live your life.

For years, Maria's grandmother wanted her to do the sensible thing: earn an MBA. In 2012, Maria was a guest speaker at Columbia Business School. On a call with her 75-year-old grandmother, it suddenly dawned on Maria:

Because of how I've structured my intellectual curiosity, they are asking me to go and talk to MBAs. I think she [grandma] really began to understand alternate ways of learning and growing.

Maria Popova is a curator.

6

THINK ENTREPRENEURIALLY

the audacity of asking

Let's begin with three stories.

In 2019, Satvik Hegde was standing in line to welcome Prime Minister Narendra Modi during his visit to Houston, Texas. Over 50,000 people had gathered to see and hear the Indian Prime Minister and the then US President Donald Trump.

As the two leaders walked past the children, Satvik stepped forward and asked for a selfie. President Trump agreed. Prime Minister Modi, who had walked a few steps ahead, turned back to join the huddle. Extending his hand, Satvik clicked the 'most powerful selfie' in the world.

The expression on the face of the girl next to Satvik told a bigger story. Her eyes widened as her hands covered her mouth.

How could Satvik have been so audacious?

Later, in a television interview, the 13-year-old was nonchalant:

> *It doesn't really hurt to ask for something that you want.*

* * *

In his early twenties, Shantanu Naidu was an automotive design engineer with Tata Elxsi in Pune. After his night shift, Shantanu would often ride his motorcycle home in the dark. One night, he saw a dog lying in a pool of blood. It had been run over many times.

Shantanu is an animal lover. Along with his friends, he made dog collars by stitching reflective material on old jeans. They then went around Pune, putting collars on all the stray dogs they could find.

One day Shantanu got a message that their reflective collar had saved a dog from being run over. Word spread. As enquires poured in, Shantanu realized he didn't have funds to make more collars. Shantanu's father suggested he write to Ratan Tata, chairman of the Tata group and a known dog lover. Shantanu debated:

> *I was hesitant at first but then I said to myself 'Why not?' So I wrote him [Mr Tata] a handwritten letter and forgot all about it.*

Two months later, Shantanu was invited to Mumbai to meet the chairman. Mr Tata agreed to fund the venture. Soon after, Shantanu left Pune to study at Cornell University.

Shantanu is now a deputy general manager at Tata Trusts, where he assists Mr Tata with philanthropic initiatives, start-up proposals, and social media.

* * *

As a kid, Steve Jobs wanted to build a frequency counter. He found the number of Bill Hewlett, the founder of Hewlett Packard (HP) in the telephone directory. When Steve called, Bill answered the phone. Twelve-year-old Steve introduced himself and asked for spare parts to build a frequency counter.

Bill was amused. Steve got the parts he wanted and an offer for an internship. He spent that summer at HP working on the assembly line for frequency counters.

Steve said:

> *I've always found something to be very true, which is*
> *most people don't get those experiences because they*
> *never ask. I have never found anybody that didn't*
> *want to help me if I asked them for help.*

* * *

What is common across the three anecdotes?

Satvik, Shantanu, and Steve all had the courage to ask for what they wanted. As the saying goes: *if you don't ask, the answer is always no.* Entrepreneurs are always asking. This chapter is about learning to think and act like an entrepreneur.

Can a movie inspire you to leave your job?

After watching Ranbir Kapoor in *Tamasha*, Anshu Mor did just that. At 44, Anshu resigned from Microsoft to become a stand-up comedian.

We will peep into Marcus Samuelsson's kitchen to find out how he blended his African roots and Swedish upbringing to become an award-winning chef. Michelle Obama selected him to cook a banquet for 400 high-profile guests at the White House.

As a student in London, Neha Kirpal enjoyed visiting galleries and art fairs. Despite little knowledge or experience of the Indian art world, she wanted to promote local artists. While on a flight to India, Neha scribbled a plan on an air sickness bag. That was the beginning of India Art Fair.

Have you seen the movie *Sully*? Imagine being a pilot of an A320 when both your engines flame out. You have lost thrust and estimate about three minutes of glide time left. The pilot of this aircraft took charge and has a lesson for us in entrepreneurial thinking.

Finally, there is Shradha Sharma, who never intended to start a business. She began YourStory without a plan or even a business model. How do you think she did it?

Doing What You Can with What You Have

Saras Sarasvathy teaches at the University of Virginia's Darden School of Business. In 2007, *Fortune Small Business* magazine named her among the top 18 entrepreneurship professors worldwide.

In her PhD thesis, Saras tried to understand how entrepreneurs think and take decisions. Working under the economist and Nobel laureate Herbert Simon, she interviewed several entrepreneurs. All of them had been in business for at least 10 years, started multiple companies, and taken at least one of them public. In her study, the entrepreneurs were given a case about a hypothetical start-up called 'Venturing' and had to take decisions to run it successfully.

At that time, it was believed that entrepreneurs first recognize an opportunity and then assemble the resources to reach their goal. However, Saras found that when faced with uncertainty, entrepreneurs adopt a different approach to decision-making. They began by assessing their personal strengths and weaknesses, and then seek to build partnerships with potential stakeholders. Entrepreneurs did not wait for the perfect solution, rather, they improvised and did what they could with what they had. Saras called this 'effectual thinking'.

The conventional approach[*] to entrepreneurship, which is the opposite of effectual thinking, centres around structured planning and prior research. This leaves little room for surprises or unexpected events. Effectual thinkers recognize that in times of uncertainty, it is difficult to plan and predict the future. They are open to surprises that can be a source of new opportunities. Rather than trying to predict the future, effectual thinkers build it by interacting with other stakeholders.

Effectual thinking is not confined to entrepreneurs. In fact, it is an approach or logic that anyone can use. Whether you are in the corporate world, government, or the social sector, effectual thinking can help you leapfrog to your goals.

	Conventional Logic	Effectual Logic
STARTING POINT	Goal oriented	Means oriented
BELIEF	Predict the future	Create the future
APPROACH	Competition	Co-creation
SURPRISES	Avoid them	Lead to new opportunities
BASIS FOR ACTION	What should I do?	What can I do?

Can this way of thinking be taught and learnt?

It was long believed that entrepreneurship was an inherent trait that you were born with. Saras disagrees. For her,

---

[*] Researchers call this a 'causal approach' to entrepreneurship.

entrepreneurship is like reading or writing, and is a skill you can develop. She quotes Jack Roseman, the tech entrepreneur:

> *Teaching entrepreneurship is like teaching music. We cannot give you a voice, but no matter what kind of voice you bring to the classroom, we can teach you to sing better.*

An Entrepreneurial Career

Anshu Mor began his new career by thinking like an entrepreneur. During his 18 years at Microsoft, Anshu had built a reputation as a master of ceremonies. He was often on stage, hosting product launches and annual company events. Anshu featured in internal brand videos and wrote content for business groups within the company. On the side, he spent time at Kommune India, which hosts workshops for artists, creators and performers.

Anshu learnt to write comedy, structure material, and perform on stage. Initially he did short gigs on other comedians' shows. Anshu became friends with Amit Tandon, a popular comedian on Netflix. Amit taught him the ropes of stand-up comedy.

A month after they met, Anshu performed at a local comedy club. He still remembers every face in the audience. As they clapped and cheered, he knew that he belonged there:

> *Strangely I was not insecure about the move at all [from Microsoft]. I guess it was because I was fairly clear on what my capabilities are . . .*

Along with three artists, Anshu set up an entertainment and storytelling collective. Besides stand-up comedy, 'Talking Mime' has a web series and hosts a podcast. Using his network, Anshu organized corporate workshops on leadership, the art of business storytelling, and brand consulting.

In his journey from corporate executive to stand-up comedian, Anshu utilized three pillars of entrepreneurial thinking: bird in hand, crazy quilt, and pilot in the plane.

Leverage the Bird in Hand

You are probably familiar with the old adage 'a bird in hand is worth two in the bush'. To think like an entrepreneur, ask yourself three questions:

- Who am I?
  List your attributes and abilities
- What do I know?
  List your education, training,
  and experience
- Whom do I know?
  List your social and professional networks

The answers will help you recognize the resources available to you and ways to use them to your advantage.

Alberto 'Beto' Perez was born in Cali, Colombia. After watching the movie *Grease*, Beto fell in love with rock and roll. He would mimic John Travolta and even dress like him at neighbourhood parties. Passionate about dancing, Beto worked multiple jobs to help his single mother support the family.

In the 1980s, Lambada was gaining popularity as a dance form. Beto took part in a national dance contest that had 3,000 participants. After winning it, he was invited to perform at clubs and got an offer to teach at a dance academy.

Learning from a Jane Fonda workout video, Beto became an aerobics instructor. One day, he accidentally left the cassettes for his usual routine at home. All he had were tapes of salsa, merengue and samba tunes recorded off the radio. That day, Beto announced a special class. He called it Zumba:

> *I started to improvise, and people started to smile.*
> *People were happy, sweating. At the end they said,*
> *'Wow! I want to do this for the rest of my life'.*

Despite a lack of fluency in English, Beto moved to Miami. Sleeping on park benches, he continued his Zumba classes. Beto got an opportunity to work with celebrities and choreographed Colombian pop star Shakira's album.

One day Beto auditioned for a job as a gym instructor. A participant in his class was from Colombia and wanted him to meet her 25-year-old son, Alberto Perlman. Alberto brought along a friend, Alberto Aghion. The two Albertos persuaded Beto to start a business with them. They called their dance company Zumba Fitness.

From the initial meeting with his co-founders, Beto discovered new opportunities:

> *As you start your career, and even once you start to find success, a lot of people will want to talk to you. You never know where one of these meetings can lead.*

The founders filmed an infomercial in a garage with a bedsheet as a backdrop. The initial idea was to sell fitness DVDs but their funds were soon exhausted. Meanwhile, some participants approached Beto to teach them to become Zumba instructors. Despite the risk of creating their own competition, they began train-the-trainer sessions. Two hundred and fifty people signed up for the first programme.

Zumba is now a global phenomenon with over 15 million practitioners. Besides fitness classes, the company has Zumba Wear, a line of accessories, and has launched a Nintendo Wii game. On a visit to Mumbai in 2015, Beto led a masterclass for over a thousand instructors. During the session he used the track 'Chittiyan Kaliyan', which was part of his personal workout routine.

* * *

Beto's approach of adapting to circumstances is what many entrepreneurs do. In a survey of Inc. 500 founders, 60 per cent did not write a business plan before launching their companies; only 12 per cent had undertaken market research and 65 per cent said they had strayed significantly from the original idea. When the future is uncertain and difficult to predict, you need to do what is doable by leveraging the bird in hand.

* * *

Now let's follow Marcus Samuelsson's culinary journey. He started by cooking for the dogs of the chef he was training under.

Born in Ethiopia, Marcus lost his mother to tuberculosis at an early age. The family was separated during the Ethiopian Civil War. Marcus and his sister were later adopted by a Swedish couple from Gothenburg.

Growing up, Marcus liked fishing and watching his adoptive grandmother work in the kitchen. Marcus loved food and enjoyed cooking with local produce. Wanting to become a chef, Marcus apprenticed in Switzerland, Austria, and France before eventually moving to the US. In *Yes Chef: A Memoir,* Marcus describes his struggles as a dark-skinned chef in Europe. On one occasion, a senior chef he was working with fed the food he had cooked to his dogs.

Marcus joined Acquit, a reputed Scandinavian restaurant in Manhattan. Soon after that, the restaurant's executive chef passed away. Marcus was given charge till a permanent replacement could be found. In short order, Marcus changed the menu and the type of cuisine the restaurant served.

Within a few months, Acquit got a three-star review from the *New York Times*, making 24-year-old Marcus the youngest chef to get this honour. He has received other recognitions including 'Best Chef in New York' by the James Beard Foundation and 'Young Global Leader' by the World Economic Forum. In 2010, the Obama administration was hosting its first official state dinner at the White House. It was in honour of Indian Prime Minister Manmohan Singh. Marcus was selected to curate and cook for the banquet.

How did Marcus make the transition from living in a shed in rural Ethiopia to being on the lawns of the White House?

Marcus took advantage of his background of being Ethiopian by birth, Swedish by upbringing, and American by choice to his advantage. In *The Medici Effect*, Frans Johannsson credits Marcus's cuisine to his ability to tear down the barriers of traditional cooking. His food combinations are unique as he connects different concepts across cultures. Marcus now owns Red Rooster, a restaurant in Harlem, where he lives among aromas and flavours from across the world:

> *I have had a long-lasting love affair with the flavours from Japan and the hustling New York street vendors. And of course a life-changing return to Ethiopia has made huge impacts on my life in food.*

A bird in hand will remind you of another maxim: 'when life throws you lemons, make lemonade'. An entrepreneurial way of thinking welcomes surprises, treating them as an opportunity to reimagine and rethink the path ahead.

Stich a Crazy Quilt

Remember the three degrees of separation from Chapter 2?

We are influenced by our friends, their friends, and their friends' friends who we may not even know. It is only beyond the three degrees of separation that their influence wanes.

A study on obesity by Yale University professor and sociologist Nicholas Christakis found that having a friend who is obese increases your risk of obesity by 57 per cent. If your friend's friend is obese, it increases the risk by 25 per cent, and having a friend whose friends' friend is obese increases the risk by 10 per cent. This is the power our networks and social groups can exert on us.

The crazy quilt pillar is about developing a network and building partnerships. Networks provide information on resource availability (*who owns what?*) and access (*who knows whom?*).

How can networks help you when you are looking for a job?

We tend to make friends with people who are like us and share similar interests. We develop strong ties by frequently keeping in touch, sharing information, and socializing with them.

Mark Granovetter, then a professor at Johns Hopkins University and now at Stanford University, studied how ideas spread among groups. Mark interviewed people who had switched jobs in the past five years. He discovered that most of them had found out about their new job from a person with whom they had only occasional contact. This is a *weak tie*. Mark's findings seem logical because your strong ties are likely to know the same people and have access to similar information that you do.

Does this mean you can ignore your strong ties?

On the contrary, we need both strong and weak ties. There is a lesson we can learn from early Indian and Chinese immigrants to Silicon Valley. These entrepreneurs initially needed support and guidance. Their strong ties helped them acquire the financial, technical, and other resources to establish themselves. As they gradually settled in, and extended their networks, they began to serve as strong ties for new immigrants.

Entrepreneurs continually need access to novel information, which their strong ties may not have. It is from their weak ties, who are in different networks, that they learn about new opportunities. This cycle of *exploiting* current opportunities and *exploring* new ones repeats itself, especially among serial entrepreneurs.

* * *

In the 1990s, Indians were viewed as good managers, not as entrepreneurs. This has changed. The Indus Entrepreneurs (TiE), described as the most successful networking organization in the world, has a role to play in this. TiE is a non-profit that helps newcomers from South Asia in their entrepreneurial journey. In class we use the abbreviation OPR (other people's resources) to describe how entrepreneurs are adept at leveraging them.

Satish Gupta is an industry veteran and a founding member of TiE. After working with IBM for 23 years across different functions, he joined a start-up:

> *What we see in Silicon Valley, especially with the new [start-up] businesses, is that contacts are everything . . . our business is to give the new person a little bit of a better start than we had.*

Engineers on the West Coast joke that Silicon Valley was built on ICs. These are not 'integrated circuits' but 'Indians and Chinese'.

* * *

The crazy quilt principle and power of networks is not confined to technology. The world of art depends on partnerships and collaborations. Neha Kirpal can show us how.

Growing up, Neha was fond of art and also intimidated by it. She found many of the museums and art galleries she visited to be cold and daunting.

She often wondered why:

> *Is there something wrong with me or the art world? My family strived hard to give me a good education: I was mad about Hindustani classical music. I was a state-level badminton player and also part of the under-19 national hockey team. Why did this [the art] world lock me out?*

Neha later moved to London, where she enjoyed visiting art galleries, fairs, and exhibitions. After a visit to Frieze, the annual art fair in London, Neha realized that art had a universal language and could be enjoyed by everyone.

Neha wanted to create an ecosystem around Indian art so that common people would have access to it. She founded the India Art Fair (IAF) in 2008. IAF showcases paintings, sculpture, and other art forms. It organized curated walkthroughs by South Asian artists. The first three editions of IAF attracted 146,000 visitors and quickly became a prominent event in the art circuit.

Did Neha start with a detailed business plan for IAF?

Well, she scribbled one on an air sickness bag during a flight from London:

> *Business plans are important and having a backup*
> *plan is important, but what's equally important is just*
> *to go with the flow. Sometimes just follow your heart,*
> *experiment, be a bit organic and take some chances.*

Partnerships and collaborations were key in Neha's effort to make art more accessible to everyone. She brought together local artists and helped them share resources and infrastructure. Without an established business model to follow, Neha created one of her own. She got the private sector on board as 'presenting partners'. Ultimately, all this served as a bridge to the international art market.

Later, Neha established partnerships with the Tate in London, the Guggenheim in New York, and the Mark Rothko Art Centre in Latvia. In 2011, IAF tied up with Angus Montgomery Arts. A partnership with MCH Basel group, which organizes 'Art Basel', followed. They curate fairs in Basel, Miami Beach, and Hong Kong. MCH Basel subsequently invested in IAF to create a joint venture.

Neha has been featured in *Fortune Magazine's* 40 under 40 and been felicitated by the World Economic Forum as a Young Global Leader. She feels that her background, and being an outsider in the art world, have worked to her advantage.

In 2018, Neha sold her stake in IAF to MCH Basel and moved on to her next start-up, which is a tech-led mental health platform. This time Neha has started her entrepreneurial journey by partnering with global scientists and policy experts to provide easy access to health solutions.

Be the Pilot in the Plane

The third pillar of entrepreneurial thinking relies on agency, which is the power to choose. Let's see how a corporate executive, a novelist, a yogi, and an entrepreneur piloted their planes.

i. The corporate executive had worked across many roles and geographies and at 38, became the CEO of Discovery Channel. Despite frequent time off for personal growth, his career did not suffer. On one sabbatical, he travelled by train and bus across Europe while sleeping in stations and hostel dormitories at night. Taking the first sabbatical had been difficult; the rest were easier. Each time he returned refreshed and energized.

ii. The novelist had never written a creative word or felt the urge to do so. That is, until he backpacked across Bolivia, Peru, and Bhutan and came back thinking of a boundary-less world. Harper Collins published his first novel. He spent six months at an artists' retreat in Portugal, mulling over a second one. It was another bestseller. His three novels sold 200,000 copies.

iii. The yogi had been inclined towards meditation since his 20s. His journey began in an ashram in south India where he learnt hatha yoga and practised vipassana. Moving to the Himalayas, he got used to cold water baths in winter and sleeping on the floor. This taught him austerity and gave him a sense of liberation.

iv. The entrepreneur had little experience of the start-up world. He had an urge to create but didn't want to be bogged down by any goal. Keen to experience 'creation in its purest form', he founded an ed-tech company. Eighteen months later he sold it for 300 million dollars. The entrepreneur worked as the CEO of the merged entity for a year. Wanting to become a 'zero again', he left in search of new pastures.

Now let's meet the pilots in these stories: the corporate executive, the novelist, the yogi, and the entrepreneur. Karan Bajaj is the protagonist of all four.

The son of an army officer, Karan studied in schools across the country. This iterant lifestyle influenced his career choices and the path he later followed. After an engineering degree, Karan did an MBA and joined Procter & Gamble.

Four years later, he left to travel around Eastern Europe, South America, and Mongolia. The experience was rich and transformative. Karan returned a year later during the financial crisis:

> *I had actually taken all my savings and spent it on travelling. So, I came back with no money, no job prospects, and I was living on my sister's couch in the living room. I later realized I had lived my worst-case scenario.*

After working with Kraft Foods for a while, Karan took another break. This time he travelled with his American girlfriend across Europe. Meanwhile, his friends were rising in the corporate world, getting married, and raising families. He accepted a different destiny, telling himself that he could not be envious of those he had never sought to emulate.

His entrepreneurial journey began after reading about an insight by a NASA researcher that children were more creative than adults. Karan wondered if his four-year-old could be taught to code. Through his network, Karan raised venture capital and founded WhiteHat Jr.

In 2020, WhiteHat Jr was acquired by Byju's in a 300 million dollar all-cash deal. Reflecting on his many journeys, Karan believes that life rewards growth:

> *You play the slots every day. Sometimes it's going to hit a jackpot and sometimes it will be a bust and you don't know why and when and how . . . all I owe my life every day is the gift of full energy, and play the slots every day.*

The pilot in the plane is a metaphor for thinking in a new way, taking charge, and proactively working towards your goals. Can a pilot, who is captain of an aircraft, have a lesson for us on how to think like an entrepreneur?

Imagine you are the pilot of US Airways Flight 1549. You have 20,000 hours of experience on the A320 you are flying. Taking off from LaGuardia Airport, you are headed towards North Carolina. Three minutes after take-off, both your engines have bird hits and lose thrust.

This is the scenario that Chesley Sullenberger (Sully) and his deputy Jeffrey Skiles faced on 15 January 2009. Sully radioed air traffic control (ATC), who held all departures at bay and cleared the A320 for a return to LaGuardia. With the glide time available, Sully estimated the aircraft would not be able to make it back. ATC offered an option to land at Teterboro in New Jersey.

Sully, a retired Air Force fighter pilot, was responsible for 155 passengers and 5 crew. Monitoring the condition of the aircraft, he weighed his options. Sully realized the risk of landing short of the runway or crashing in a densely populated area.

With the clock ticking, he took charge of the controls from his co-pilot. Calling the A320 'my aircraft' he radioed ATC:

We're going to be in the Hudson.

Sully instructed the crew and passengers to brace for impact while he navigated his plane towards the Hudson River. Flying just 270 metres over the George Washington Bridge, Sully made an unpowered ditch-landing in the river.

As the plane bobbed in water, passengers were evacuated in −7°C temperatures in a rescue operation involving the US Coast Guard and firefighters. Fearing an explosion, some passengers jumped into the water and swam towards boats that had been diverted from ferrying tourists to the nearby Statue of Liberty. Others stood on the partially submerged slides and on the wings.

After all the passengers had been evacuated, Sully walked the length of the cabin and back, ensuring no one was left behind. As the pilot and captain of the aircraft, he was the last to leave.

The entire incident, from bird-hits to ditching, had taken 3 minutes and 28 seconds.

Sully had estimated a glide time of less than three minutes. Whether this was enough to return to LaGuardia or fly to Teterboro was a call only the pilot could take. There was no flying manual to prepare for such an eventuality:

No one warned us. No one said, 'you are going to lose both engines at a lower altitude than any jet in history'. But, be cool, just make a left turn for LaGuardia like you are going to pick up milk.

As depicted in the film *Sully: Miracle on the Hudson*, the National Transportation Safety Board (NTSB) did a post-analysis by making pilots fly an A320 without engine power on a simulator. They found that only half the pilots were able to return successfully to LaGuardia or land at Teterboro.

Ultimately the NTSB commended Sully, describing his decision to land in the Hudson as 'the most successful ditching in American history'.

So What?

Improvising with a bird in hand, leveraging partnerships with a crazy quilt and taking charge as the pilot in the plane are three pillars that will help you think like an entrepreneur. Let's see how these worked for someone who never intended to start a business but nevertheless did so.

Shradha Sharma is from Patna, where many youngsters dream of studying in Delhi. She worked hard and made it to St Stephen's College. While at college, Shradha wanted to join the debating society. She was rejected for lacking the 'Shakespearean style' of debating.

On her next visit home, Shradha confronted her former schoolteacher. Why had the school failed to teach her the right tone, diction, and art of rebuttal?

Her teacher's response has stayed with her:

> *Whatever you did not get, whatever you were deprived of, whatever you think you lack, your constraint, whatever you think as a Bihari kid you were not given will be your biggest strength.*

Shradha began working with the *Times of India* and CNBC, where she wrote stories on entrepreneurs and their start-ups. One day, an entrepreneur she was speaking with broke into tears as his story had not been published.

Shradha founded YourStory, an online platform to promote stories of lesser-known entrepreneurs. She began her entrepreneurial journey in 2008 without a plan, financial projections, or a marketing strategy:

> *It's not that I wanted to run a business. That was not the reason I started. There was no business model. [I thought] business model I will figure out, revenue model I will figure out.*

YourStory received angel funding from Ratan Tata and others in 2015. This was a signal for the venture capital community who invested in subsequent rounds.

Thinking entrepreneurially could help you make decisions while being surrounded by uncertainty, change your career, or even start a venture.

As a bachelor in Bengaluru, Priyank (author) had a different challenge:

> *My apartment in Indira Nagar was frequented by friends and colleagues. I was always keen to cook for them. There were two ways to showcase my limited culinary skills. I could find out everyone's food preferences, buy the ingredients, and follow directions from an online recipe. Alternately, I could use ingredients available in the kitchen and surprise them with a noisy cook-out.*

A curry-in-a-hurry.

What would you do?

A TOOLKIT

your personal journey map

Men wanted for hazardous journey.
Low wages, bitter cold,
long hours of complete darkness.
Safe return doubtful.
Honour and recognition in event of success.

Legend has it that Irish explorer Sir Ernest Henry Shackleton ran this advertisement in a London newspaper in December 1913. He needed volunteers for his Imperial Trans-Antarctic expedition. Five thousand men responded. 'Three sporty girls' also wrote in wanting to be part of the expedition. They were prepared to wear men's clothes if needed.

To raise funds, Shackleton announced a detailed plan for the expedition. His team would be the first to cross the entire Antarctic continent on foot. Two ships would set sail for different destinations. Shackleton, and six men comprising the shore party, would head to Vahsel Bay. They would then trek 2,900 kilometres on the white continent. Due to limits on what could be hauled, the second ship would drop off supplies that Shackleton's group would pick up on the way.

Endurance and its crew, with 69 dogs in tow, set sail in 1915. The ship's carpenter brought his cat on board. Named Mrs Chippy, she would follow him around like an 'overly attentive wife'. A month into the voyage, it was discovered that Mrs Chippy was male, but the name stuck.

Plans went awry when about 100 miles from its destination, Endurance was trapped in shifting ice. The ship and its crew would remain stationary till the ice melted the following spring. Boilers were shut down and for many months the ship remained adrift.

Shackleton realized that his crew were more likely to perish from boredom than lack of food. He set a routine for them. Crew members were assigned tasks like looking for seal or penguin meat, swabbing decks, and searching for navigable breaks in the ice. There were leisure activities, including soccer and dog sled races on which the men wagered bets of chocolates and cigarettes.

As spring approached, the ice began to melt and break off. Unfortunately, ice movements over the winter had damaged the ship's hull and it began to take in water. Endurance had to be abandoned. Using battered timber from the ship, the crew set up an ocean camp on the sea ice. There, they stocked food supplies and lifeboats that had been salvaged.

Gradually Endurance began to slip beneath the ice. Shackleton stayed awake the night it sank. Next morning, after coffee had been served to the crew, in a calm voice he announced:

Ship and stores have gone, so now we'll go home.

After having been at sea and marooned on ice floes for 497 days, the entire crew returned home safely. Earlier, Shackleton and a few men had set sail in a lifeboat to reach the nearest whaling station. After several unsuccessful attempts, he returned to rescue his crew. Although close to death, all the men in the expedition went home. Sadly, the dogs and Mrs Chippy did not make it.

A voyage of adventure and discovery had become a test of human endurance. It has been described as one of the greatest stories in the annals of exploration. Shackleton was knighted and became a hero in Britain.

How did Shackleton manage to get his entire crew home safely?

Shackleton had a goal (to make it through the winter), knew his strengths (a well-trained and motivated crew), and weaknesses (cold nights and months in darkness). He knew the challenge ahead (ensure hopelessness did not set in) and steps to reach his goal.

This story of ordinary men confronting extraordinary circumstances is a popular case that is taught in business schools. The lessons from Shackleton's journey can be summed up in three words:

Have a plan.

The toolkit in this chapter will help you make a plan to reach your goals.

The Start-Up of You

A Business Model Canvas (BMC) is a strategic tool to conceptualize and explain the various elements of a venture. It is popular in Silicon Valley with both venture capitalists and start-ups. In a class exercise we make our students think of a venture they might start and fill the nine boxes of a BMC describing their proposal.

Based on the numerous BMCs we have seen over the years and our personal experience of mentoring entrepreneurs, we have crafted a Personal Journey Map (PJM). This is a toolkit with six boxes for you to reflect on, plan, and execute the steps to achieve your goals. To borrow from Reid Hoffman, the founder of LinkedIn, it is a pictorial representation of *the start-up of you*.

Remember the word start-up is a subject, object, and verb at the same time. A start-up is defined as the 'action or process of setting something into motion'. We interpret that as having a goal and taking steps to achieve it.

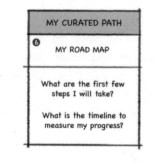

MY CURRENT REPERTOIRE		
❶ GOALS & AMBITIONS	❷ EXISTING PORTFOLIO	❸ GAPS & ROADBLOCKS
What are my goals? What do I value?	What are my strengths and weaknesses? What do I like doing & what am I good at?	What do I need to overcome to achieve my goals? What prevents me from reaching them?

THE LANDSCAPE AHEAD	
❹ NEW OPPORTUNITIES	❺ CHANGE COMMITMENT
What advantages do I have in the current environment? What steps do I need to take to achieve my goals?	What sacrifices do I need to make to achieve my goals? What are my opportunity costs?

MY CURATED PATH
❻ MY ROAD MAP
What are the first few steps I will take? What is the timeline to measure my progress?

Your PJM has three sections:

a) My Current Repertoire
b) The Landscape Ahead
c) My Curated Path

The boxes in My Current Repertoire are your goals and ambitions, your existing portfolio, and the gaps and roadblocks you might encounter in reaching your goals. The Landscape Ahead will help you visualize new opportunities and think about a change commitment you need to achieve your goals. Finally, My Curated Path will help you find a way to reach your destination.

The boxes in the PJM are linked. As you fill them up, you will see their interconnectedness. Remember the PJM is a live document that you should revisit at regular intervals.

The next section explains the individual elements of the PJM and how they align with some of the 6 practices and 18 pillars you have encountered in this book.

My Current Repertoire

This section is about your purpose. In the Japanese concept of 'ikigai', 'iki' means life and 'gai' is result or worth. It is about the balance you strike between what you are good at, what you love, what the world needs, and what you can be paid for. A growth mindset will guide the discovery of your ikigai.

Box 1: Goals and Ambitions

Your goals should be SMART: specific, meaningful, achievable, relevant, and time bound. Evaluate them periodically and make changes when needed. After achieving goals, you have prioritized, you can set new ones for yourself. Remember Warren Buffet's 5/25 rule and focus on the essential.

Box 2: Existing Portfolio

The Temple of Apollo in Delphi, Greece, has an inscription in its forecourt: 'Know thyself'. This directive has a larger purpose. We need to understand ourselves before we can engage meaningfully with the outside world.

To know yourself, use an effectual approach by asking:

- Who am I?
  (my attributes and abilities)
- What do I know?
  (my education, training, experience)
- Whom do I know?
  (my social and professional networks)

Begin with a bird in hand and create networks using the crazy quilt principle.

Box 3: Gaps and Roadblocks

To recognize your gaps and roadblocks, you need to be intellectually humble and accept limits to what you know. Remember the toilet test and how many people overestimated their understanding of a flush toilet.

While thinking about your goals and ambitions, examine your portfolio. Identify what you lack and the steps needed to achieve your goals. Your roadblocks may be financial, educational, or due to societal pressures. Assess your abilities against those of someone you want to emulate. Seek help from a mentor, confidant or even a professional coach.

The Landscape Ahead

Did you know that the game of snakes and ladders originated in ancient India?

It was known as *Mokshapat*. Invented in the 13th century, the game was used as moral instruction for children. In *Mokshapat*, the boxes with ladders stood for virtues while the snakes represented vices.

Imagine you are playing this game. There is a starting point (your current position), an ultimate objective (goals and ambitions), the likelihood of meeting snakes (weaknesses and roadblocks) and discovering ladders (strengths and surprises). And just like the numbers you get when you roll dice, there will be factors beyond your control that you will need to accept.

Box 4: New Opportunities

How do you seek opportunities in a VUCA (volatile, uncertain, complex, and ambiguous) world?

At work, listen to your customers, suppliers, vendors, and consultants. Pay attention to what they like and dislike. Find out where are they investing their time and resources. Social media can be a source of information about new opportunities.

Subscribe to industry publications, join associations, and follow content curators. Learn about new domains, their techniques, and trends. They may point to new opportunities. Just like digital humanities, there are new interdisciplinary fields in which you can be an early mover.

Box 5: Change Commitment

This is about your commitment and the sacrifices you are prepared to make to achieve them. Develop grit and learn to deal with boredom.

My Curated Path

Have you heard of *Chaturanga*?

Modern-day chess traces its origins to this board game that was played in India in the 15th century. It included four elements of the ancient Indian army—infantry, cavalry, elephants, and chariots.

Think of your journey as a game of chess with several pieces to move. Given their position on the board and the rules of the game, you must consider your next move while keeping in mind your long-term objective.

Box 6: My Road Map

The final box details a step-by-step approach to reach your destination. You are the pilot of your plane. As you craft your road map, remember to develop grit and also nudge yourself. To track your progress, put a timeline to every step.

The appendix contains PJMs of a few of our students. It might help you fill yours.

EPILOGUE

a late bloomer

At any given age, you're getting better at some things, you're getting worse at some things and you're plateauing at some others. There's probably no one age at which you're peaking at most things, much less all of them.

—Richard Karlgaard

One night, during hourly patrols of a parking yard for rental trucks he oversaw, Richard Karlgaard heard a menacing sound. Walking towards the fence, he pointed his flashlight at the next-door plot. Staring back at him was a rottweiler.* In that moment, it dawned on Richard that his colleague and competitor at work was a watchdog.

Richard studied at Stanford University, where he had opted for a 'mickey mouse curriculum'. This pejorative term describes a course that is worthless or irrelevant. After graduation, Richard

---

* A muscular breed of dog often used as a guard.

held a series of short-term jobs: typist, dishwasher, and finally, night watchman.

Then something changed.

As Richard describes it, his brain suddenly woke up. After a job as a writer, he co-founded *Upside Magazine*, Silicon Valley's first business publication in 1989. Three years later Richard, along with Steve Forbes, launched *Forbes ASAP*. At 44, he became the publisher of *Forbes Magazine*.

During this time, Richard got married, learnt to fly a plane, and wrote six books. *Life 2.0*, published in 2004, is a bestseller and led him to a speaking career that has taken him around the world.

Richard is a late bloomer.

Many of us in our twenties, thirties, and even later feel we lack direction. Sociologists describe this as 'the changing timetable for adulthood'.

Film director Satyajit Ray was 34 when he made his first film, *Pather Panchali*. It won 11 international awards. Writer Nirad Chaudhuri failed his MA exams. At 54, he wrote his first book *The Autobiography of an Unknown Indian*, an account of Bengal's Hindu aristocracy. It is a classic in its genre. Fauja Singh began running marathons at 89. He clocked his best time of six hours and two minutes at the Toronto Waterfront Marathon when he was 92.

So, if you have not yet sold your first start-up, become the CEO of a company, or created the impact you had dreamt of, do not worry.

Late bloomers can leapfrog.

APPENDIX

*personal journey maps
of our students*[*]

---

[*] Names have been changed to protect their privacy.

Sabah Ali (23)

Sabah, who majored in economics from a liberal arts university, enjoys working with numbers. She wants to be the CEO of a multinational company. To reach that goal, Sabah would like to do an MBA, preferably in Europe. Meanwhile, she plans to live and work in France. Sabah is trying to perfect the pronunciation of her favourite dish, *ratatouille*; she is proud of her ability to say *bon appétit* perfectly.

Sabah's PJM

MY CURRENT REPERTOIRE		
❶ GOALS & AMBITIONS	**❷ EXISTING PORTFOLIO**	**❸ GAPS & ROADBLOCKS**
CEO of an MNC in the next 20 years	Degree in economics	Can't speak and read French fluently
Get admitted to a top international business school	Aptitude for learning languages	Lack of finance skills
Work in France	Have friends and family in Paris	Family not comfortable with letting me travel alone

THE LANDSCAPE AHEAD	
❹ NEW OPPORTUNITIES	**❺ CHANGE COMMITMENT**
Emerging career opportunities in the UK	Learn French
English speaking professionals in demand in Europe	Find a mentor

MY CURATED PATH
❻ MY ROAD MAP
Join French classes by next month
Get aunt's help to convince family
Request a mentoring call with a professor

Rahul Jain (41)

Rahul has founded an ecotourism
company in Leh, Ladakh, which
trends on TripAdvisor.
This is his third career
change. After working in
digital transformation for a
decade, Rahul tried his hand
at gastronomy and mixology,
by starting a bar on Residency
Road in Bengaluru. Rahul is a
fitness enthusiast and wants to
make his current venture a global
ecotourism company.

Rahul's PJM

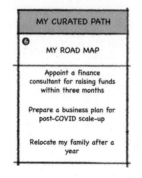

MY CURRENT REPERTOIRE

❶ GOALS & AMBITIONS	❷ EXISTING PORTFOLIO	❸ GAPS & ROADBLOCKS
Scale start-up across 12 locations in India in the next three years	Proficient at sales and operations	Lack of access to funds and potential B2B customers
Take my start-up global in five years	Comfortable in dealing with uncertainty	Shuttling between two cities as my family lives in Delhi

THE LANDSCAPE AHEAD

❹ NEW OPPORTUNITIES	❺ CHANGE COMMITMENT
Emerging business models of personal micro-mobility	I am willing to live away from my family for a year
Growing EV (electric vehicle) market and ecosystem	Committing up to 18 hours/day to the start-up

MY CURATED PATH

❻ MY ROAD MAP
Appoint a finance consultant for raising funds within three months
Prepare a business plan for post-COVID scale-up
Relocate my family after a year

Aditi Mathai (33)

Aditi founded an ed-tech venture that introduces entrepreneurship to university students. Both her start-up and her son are two years old; she loves them equally. Aditi aims to join the Travelers Century Club by visiting 100 countries. At some stage she would like to do a PhD. Currently, she wants to scale her start-up.

Aditi's PJM

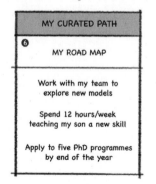

MY CURRENT REPERTOIRE

❶ GOALS & AMBITIONS	❷ EXISTING PORTFOLIO	❸ GAPS & ROADBLOCKS
Develop entrepreneurship among university students	Good presentation and writing skills	Balance work, education and raising a naughty two-year old
Complete a PhD	Enjoy networking	A habitual procrastinator
Travel to 100 countries in the world	Love travelling and don't mind living out of a suitcase	Time management

THE LANDSCAPE AHEAD

❹ NEW OPPORTUNITIES	❺ CHANGE COMMITMENT
Emerging travel business models	Step out of comfort zone and stop believing that I am already doing enough
Virtual experiential learning and internships	Develop a research mindset

MY CURATED PATH

❻ MY ROAD MAP
Work with my team to explore new models
Spend 12 hours/week teaching my son a new skill
Apply to five PhD programmes by end of the year

Vir Kapoor (26)

An electrical and electronics engineer,
Vir worked as a software developer
before moving to Mumbai for a
career in Bollywood. He has been
active in the theatre circuit and has auditioned
for a few films. Unsure if he was on the right path,
Vir enrolled in a master's programme in liberal
arts. He would now like another attempt at an
acting career and views the proliferation of OTT
platforms as an opportunity.

Vir's PJM

MY CURRENT REPERTOIRE		
❶ GOALS & AMBITIONS	**❷ EXISTING PORTFOLIO**	**❸ GAPS & ROADBLOCKS**
Be recognised as a versatile actor in Bollywood films	Excellent stage presence in theatre	Lack of financial support from family
Work with Karan Johar	Done modelling assignments with celebrities	No godfather or mentors in the film industry

THE LANDSCAPE AHEAD	
❹ NEW OPPORTUNITIES	**❺ CHANGE COMMITMENT**
Growth of OTT platforms and low-budget content	Improve dance skills with coaching
Demand for actors by European and Asian production houses after success of Korean dramas such as *Squid Games*	Make long-distance relationship work with my girlfriend

MY CURATED PATH
❻ MY ROAD MAP
Identify top Asian and European production houses and send my portfolio to them in the next six months
Attend weekend dance classes for a year
Conduct three online improv classes every month to supplement income

My PJM

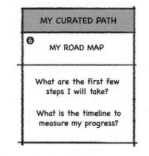

MY CURRENT REPERTOIRE		
❶ GOALS & AMBITIONS	**❷ EXISTING PORTFOLIO**	**❸ GAPS & ROADBLOCKS**
What are my goals? What do I value?	What are my strengths and weaknesses? What do I like doing & what am I good at?	What do I need to overcome to achieve my goals? What prevents me from reaching them?

THE LANDSCAPE AHEAD	
❹ NEW OPPORTUNITIES	**❺ CHANGE COMMITMENT**
What advantages do I have in the current environment? What steps do I need to take to achieve my goals?	What sacrifices do I need to make to achieve my goals? What are my opportunity costs?

MY CURATED PATH
❻ MY ROAD MAP
What are the first few steps I will take? What is the timeline to measure my progress?

MY CURRENT REPERTOIRE		
❶ GOALS & AMBITIONS	❷ EXISTING PORTFOLIO	❸ GAPS & ROADBLOCKS

THE LANDSCAPE AHEAD	
❹ NEW OPPORTUNITIES	❺ CHANGE COMMITMENT

MY CURATED PATH
❻ MY ROAD MAP

A downloadable version of the PJM and additional resources about the six practices are available on our website

www.leapfrog.work

NOTES AND REFERENCES

'Pracademic', a word often used in the world of entrepreneurship education, has yet to find its way into the English dictionary. It is an abridgment of 'practitioner-academic', someone who is both an academic and a practitioner at the same time. Pracademics help to bridge the academic and professional worlds and draw links between theory and practice.

As pracademics, we have championed ideas by using anecdotes from the world of practice. Many of these stories are validated by published research; others are drawn from our own experience and that of our students who shared them with us. In academia, scholarship is evaluated, critiqued, and sometimes even refuted by fellow researchers, leaving its interpretation to the astute reader. As authors, we have cited research that supports our ideas and has helped us establish connections with the world of practice.

Introduction

Page   **Citation**

vii   **A banana republic**
A banana republic is a derogatory term, often used to describe a politically unstable country or region.
Longley R, 'What Is a Banana Republic? Definition and Examples,' *ThoughtCo*, November 19, 2019.

vii   **That year Honduras was hit by Hurricane Mitch**
Kumar D, 'Coronavirus Impact: Why the Idea of Diversification Is Looking Like the Old Bridge on River Choluteca,' *Economic Times*, August 12, 2020.

vii   **The river had altered its course**
Iyer P, 'The Bridge on the River Choluteca,' *Business World*, August 23, 2020.

viii   **Today, our mantra can no longer**
Collins J and Porras J, '*Built to Last: Successful Habits of Visionary Companies*,' Penguin Random House, 2005.

viii   **Leapfrog is a concept in industrial organizations**
Yayboke E, Carter WA, and Crumpler W, 'The Need for a Leapfrog Strategy,' Centre for Strategic and International Studies, April 10, 2020.

viii   **Economists tell us that leapfrogging**
Brezis E and Krugman P, 'Technology and Life Cycle of Cities,' *Journal of Economic Growth* 2(4), 1997, 369–383.

Chapter 1 – Develop Grit

2   **They are winners of the Scripps National Spelling Bee**
PTI, 'Indian-Americans Aim to Maintain Dominance in US Spelling Bee,' *Economic Times*, May 23, 2013.
Mervosh S, '3 of This Year's Spelling Bee Winners Are Friends from Dallas,' *New York Times*, May 31, 2019.

2   **In 2019, 11 million children competed**
CNN Editorial Research, 'National Spelling Bee Fast Facts,' CNN, July 9, 2021.

2   **The Spelling Bee's popularity rivals**
Anecdotes on the Spelling Bee are from the following sources:
ESPN, 'Great Moments in Spelling Bee History,' ESPN, June 5, 2010.
Steinberg D, 'ESPN's Kevin Negandhi Gets his Dream Assignment: National Spelling Bee, a.k.a. "The Indian Super Bowl",' *The Washington Post*, June 1, 2017.
News18, 'US: Indian-American Arvind Mahankali Wins National Spelling Bee,' News18, May 31, 2013.

3   *In the Netflix documentary* **Spelling the Dream**
Rega S, director, '*Spelling the Dream*,' Netflix, 2020.

3   *The only way the Indian American kids are losing*
Ibid.

4   *We're throwing the dictionary at you*
Fitzgerald M. 'In a Historic Finale, 8 Spellers Just Won the 2019 Scripps National Spelling Bee,' *Time Magazine*, May 31, 2019.

4   *Meanwhile, the winners had coined a new word*
Zarrell M, '8 Winners of 2019 Scripps National Spelling Bee Coin Term for Themselves: Octochamps,' ABC News, May 31, 2019.

4   *In 2022, Harini Logan of Texas*
Goldberg B, 'U.S. National Spelling Bee Champ Is Harini Logan of Texas in Historic Win,' *Reuters*, June 4, 2022.

5   *I saw and heard how, when he was made to listen*
Deutsch D, 'The Puzzle of Absolute Pitch,' *Current Directions in Psychological Science* 11(6), 2002, 200-204.

5   *Mozart was believed to be born with perfect*
McCall R, 'Brain Differences Could Be the Secret to Mozart's Perfect Pitch,' *IFL Science*, February 12, 2019.
https://www.iflscience.com/brain-differences-could-be-the-secret-to-mozarts-perfect-pitch-51520
(Accessed: July 27, 2022).

6   *Less than 1 in 10,000 musicians*
Deutsch D, Henthorn T, Marvin E, and Hong Shuai X, 'Absolute Pitch among American and Chinese Conservatory Students: Prevalence Differences, and Evidence for a Speech-Related Critical Period,' *The Journal of the Acoustical Society of America* 119(2), 2006, 719-722.
Ingmire J, 'Acquiring 'Perfect' Pitch May Be Possible for Some Adults,' *University of Chicago News*, May 28, 2015.

6   *Ericsson offered a more nuanced view*
Ericsson A and Pool R, 'Peak: How All of Us Can Achieve Extraordinary Things,' Penguin Random House, 2016.

6   *In these languages, similar words have different meanings*
University of California, San Diego, 'Tone Language Is Key to Perfect Pitch,' *Science Daily*, May 20, 2009.
https://www.sciencedaily.com/releases/2009/05/090519172202.htm
(Accessed: July 27, 2022).

6   *For example, in Mandarin, the syllable 'ma'*
Gui S, 'The Four Mandarin Chinese Tones,' *ThoughtCo*, November 4, 2019.

6   ***Illustration: Chinese Tones***
         Adapted from:
         https://enjoyspeakingchinese.com/fundamentals/how-to-learn-chinese-tones
         (Accessed: July 12, 2022).

7   ***A study examined children***
         Sakakibara A, 'A Longitudinal Study of the Process of Acquiring Absolute
         Pitch: A Practical Report of Training with the 'Chord Identification Method','
         Psychology of Music 42(1), 2014, 86-111.

7   ***Well-known in that era, Bach***
         Bourdon A, 'Johann Christian Bach's Influence on Mozart's Developing Style,'
         University of Richmond Thesis, 2010.

8   ***Violinists at the Berlin Academy of Music***
         Ericsson K, Krampe R, and Tesch-Römer C, 'The Role of Deliberate Practice
         in the Acquisition of Expert Performance,' *Psychological Review* 100 (3), 1993,
         363-406.
         Kurutz S, 'Anders Ericsson, Psychologist and 'Expert on Experts', Dies at 72',
         New York Times, July 1, 2020.

9   ***Selection to West Point is competitive***
         Anecdotes on selection to West Point are from the following sources:
         Duckworth AL, '*Grit: The Power of Passion and Perseverance*,' Scribner, 2016.
         Duckworth AL, Peterson C, Matthews M, and Kelly D, 'Grit: Perseverance and
         Passion for Long-Term Goals,' *Journal of Personality and Social Psychology* 92(6),
         2007, 1087-1101.
         'America's Best College,' *Forbes*, August 6, 2009.
         Atkinson R, '*The Long Gray Line: The American Journey of West Point's Class of
         1966*,' Macmillan, 2009.
         Nothing Here, 'Beast – Story about West Point,' YouTube, May 22, 2015.
         'West Point Class Profile,' West Point, The U.S. Military Academy, 2018.
         https://www.westpoint.edu/admissions/class-profile
         (Accessed: July 12, 2022).

10   ***Sales employees with grit are more likely***
         Eskreis-Winkler L, Duckworth AL, Shulman E, and Beal S, 'The Grit Effect:
         Predicting Retention in the Military, the Workplace, School and Marriage,'
         Frontiers in Psychology 3, 2014, 5-36.

Contrarian view: While grit has been well regarded by many educationists, it has
also been criticized by some researchers. A meta-analysis of 88 studies on grit
found that it was close to conscientiousness, which is defined as being careful and
diligent, and having the desire to undertake a task well. This analysis found that
the perseverance aspect of the grit construct can help in predicting performance,
especially in settings such as higher education where student retention can be
problematic.

Credé M, Tynan M, and Harms P, 'Much Ado about Grit: A Meta-Analytic Synthesis of the Grit Literature,' *Journal of Personality and Social Psychology* 113(3), 2017, 492-511.

Bazelais P, Lemay DJ, and Doleck T, 'How Does Grit Impact College Students' Academic Achievement in Science?' *European Journal of Science and Mathematics Education* 4(1), 2016, 33-43.

10   At an Ivy League university
Duckworth AL, Peterson C, Matthews M, and Kelly D, 'Grit: Perseverance and Passion for Long-Term Goals,' *Journal of Personality and Social Psychology* 92(6), 2007, 1087-1101.

11   We know that from chess players
Duckworth AL, '*Grit: The Power of Passion and Perseverance*,' Scribner, 2016.
Eskreis-Winkler L, Duckworth AL, Shulman E, and Beal S, 'The Grit Effect: Predicting Retention in the Military, the Workplace, School and Marriage,' *Frontiers in Psychology* 3, 2014, 5-36.

11   As Peter Drucker said
Drucker J, 'You Are What You Measure,' *Forbes*, December 4, 2018.

11   A widely used grit scale has 10 questions
Duckworth AL, 'Grit Scale,', n.d.
https://angeladuckworth.com/grit-scale/
(Accessed: January 23, 2022).

11   As a reference, a grit score of 4.3
Cabral C, 'The Grit Test: Your Grit Score & What It Means,' January 7, 2021.
https://www.shortform.com/blog/grit-test/
(Accessed: July 12, 2022).

13   In Outliers: The Story of Success
Gladwell M, '*Outliers: The Story of Success*,' Little, Brown & Company, 2008.
Chase WG and Simon HA, 'Perception in Chess,' *Cognitive Psychology* 4(1), 1973, 55-81.

13   An often-quoted story is that of Shizuka Arakawa
Syed M, '*Bounce: The Myth of Talent and Power of Practice*,' HarperCollins, 2010.
Clarey C, 'Figure Skating: As Rivals Slip, Arakawa Glides to a Rare Gold,' *New York Times*, February 24, 2006.

14   Over a year, with one per cent improvement
Clear J, '*Atomic Habits: Tiny Changes, Remarkable Results: An Easy & Proven Way to Build Good Habits & Break Bad Ones*,' Penguin Random House, 2018.

14   Ericsson, the researcher whose work
Anecdote on Ericsson's experiment with SF is from the following sources:

Ericsson K, Krampe R, and Tesch-Römer C, 'The Role of Deliberate Practice in the Acquisition of Expert Performance,' *Psychological Review* 100 (3), 1993, 363-406.

Ericsson A and Pool R, *'Peak: How All of Us Can Achieve Extraordinary Things,'* Penguin Random House, 2016.

14   In Talent Is Overrated, *Geoff Colvin*

Colvin G, *'Talent Is Overrated: What Really Separates World-Class Performers from Everybody Else,'* Penguin Random House, 2010.

16   *If you practice with your fingers*

Haslop C, 'Practice: How Much Is Enough,' Violin Mastery, May 12, 2007. https://violinmastery.com/practice-how-much-is-enough/ (Accessed: August 8, 2022).

Ericsson KA, Prietula MJ, and Cokely ET, 'The Making of an Expert,' *Harvard Business Review* 85(7/8), 2007, 114–121.

17   *Unwilling to leave the skating rink*

Colvin G, *'Talent Is Overrated: What Really Separates World-Class Performers from Everybody Else,'* Penguin Random House, 2010.

Contrarian view: While Malcolm Gladwell popularized the 10,000-hour rule in his book *Outliers: The Story of Success,* other researchers, including Ericsson, have also critiqued it.

Goleman D, *'Focus: The Hidden Driver of Excellence,'* Harper Collins, 2013.

Sample I, 'Blow to 10,000-Hour Rule as Study Finds Practice Doesn't Always Make Perfect,' *The Guardian*, August 21, 2019.

17   *Nikolai changed Shizuka's music and routine*

Clarey C, 'Intertwined Quests for the Elusive Gold,' *International Herald Tribune*, February 23, 2006.

18   *Elite skaters differ from sub-elites*

Ericsson KA, Prietula MJ, and Cokely ET, 'The Making of an Expert,' *Harvard Business Review* 85(7/8), 2007, 114–121.

Ericsson KA, Roring RW, and Nandagopal K, 'Giftedness and Evidence for Reproducibly Superior Performance: An Account Based on the Expert Performance Framework,' *High Ability Studies* 18(1), 2007, 3-56.

18   *They also focus on those jumps and combinations*

Deakin, JM and Cobley S, 'An Examination of the Practice Environments in Figure Skating and Volleyball: A Search for Deliberate Practice,' Expert Performance in Sports: *Advances in Research on Sport Expertise*, 2003, 90-113.

18   *Our brains have an in-built navigational system*

Epstein RA, Patai EZ, Julian JB, and Spiers HJ, 'The Cognitive Map in Humans: Spatial Navigation and Beyond,' *Nature Neuroscience* 20(11), 2017, 1504-1513.

Ericsson KA and Pool R, *'Peak: How All of Us Can Achieve Extraordinary Things,'* Penguin Random House, 2016.

Constantinescu AO, O'Reilly JX, and Behrens TEJ, 'Organizing Conceptual Knowledge in Humans with a Grid-Like Code,' *Science* 352(6292), 2016, 1464-1468.

19   *Experts develop complex mental images*
Ericsson KA and Harwell KW, 'Deliberate Practice and Proposed Limits on the Effects of Practice on the Acquisition of Expert Performance: Why the Original Definition Matters and Recommendations for Future Research,' *Frontiers in Psychology* 10, 2019, 1-19.

19   *Expert chess players often play multiple boards*
Chase WG and Simon HA, 'Perception in Chess,' *Cognitive Psychology* 4(1), 1973, 55-81.
De Groot AD, '*Thought and Choice in Chess,*' De Gruyter Mouton, 2014.

20   *We all have a natural tendency*
Gobet F, 'Chunking Models of Expertise: Implications for Education,' *Applied Cognitive Psychology* 19(2), 2005, 183-204.

20   *Michael Phelps, one of the most decorated swimmers*
'Biography: Michael Phelps,' Olympics, 2022.
https://olympics.com/en/athletes/michael-phelps-ii
(Accessed: July 12, 2022).

20   *I could not see the line at the bottom of the pool*
Phelps M and Abrahamson A, *'No Limits: The Will to Succeed,'* Simon and Schuster, 2008.

20   *Phelps and his coach Bob Bowman*
Futterman M, 'Michael Phelps's Coach Shares His Secrets,' *Wall Street Journal*, May 12, 2016.

20   *At the end of each practice, Bowman would*
Duhigg C, '*The Power of Habit: Why We Do What We Do in Life and Business,*' Penguin Random House, 2012.

21   *Recently, a student told us about Holly Thompson*
Ellicott C, 'Bored Stiff: Student Yawned So Hard During Lecture That She Couldn't Close Her Mouth,' *Daily Mail*, April 9, 2011.
Meidyboi, 'Holly Thompson – Yawning in Class, This Girl Can't Shut Her Mouth' YouTube, April 14, 2011.

22   *However, even professional, amateur, and college athletes*
Velasco F and Jorda R, 'Portrait of Boredom among Athletes and Its Implications in Sports Management: A Multi-Method Approach,' *Frontiers in Psychology* 11, 2020, 1-12.

22   *In* Atomic Habits, *James Clear*
Clear J, '*Atomic Habits: Tiny Changes, Remarkable Results: An Easy & Proven Way to Build Good Habits & Break Bad Ones,*' Penguin Random House, 2018.

22 *While practising, participants used three strategies*
Duckworth AL, Kirby TA, Tsukayama E, Berstein H, and Ericsson KA, 'Deliberate Practice Spells Success: Why Grittier Competitors Triumph at the National Spelling Bee,' *Social Psychological and Personality Science* 2(2), 2011, 174–181.

23 *Grandma's phonetic pronunciation of words*
Guo A, 'Competition Preparation and Deliberate Practice: A Study of the 2005 National Spelling Bee Finalists,' The University of Toledo, Doctoral Dissertation, 2006.

23 *When you mastered it*
Ibid.

23 *You might have more talent than me*
Dobuzinskis A, 'Will Smith Leads Forbes Star Bankability List,' *Reuters*, February 11, 2009.

24 *A Harvard University study on psychological health*
Vaillant GE, '*Triumphs of Experience: The Men of the Harvard Grant Study,*' Harvard University Press, 2012.

25 *Time spent on the treadmill was found*
Lawton E, Brymer E, Clough P, and Denovan A, 'The Relationship between the Physical Activity Environment, Nature Relatedness, Anxiety, and the Psychological Well-Being Benefits of Regular Exercisers,' *Frontiers in Psychology* 8, 2017, 1-11.

Chapter 2 – Nudge Yourself

29 *Spillage reduced by 80 per cent*
Ingraham C, 'What's a Urinal Fly, and What Does It Have to do with Winning a Nobel Prize?' *Washington Post*, October 9, 2017.
Sommer J, 'When Humans Need a Nudge toward Rationality,' *New York Times*, February 7, 2009.

30 *Richard Thaler, winner of the 2017 Nobel Prize*
Thaler RH and Sunstein CR, '*Nudge: Improving Decisions about Health, Wealth, and Happiness,*' Penguin Random House, 2009.
A revised edition of this book, sub-titled 'The Final Edition,' was published in 2021.
Ahmed K, 'Nudge Economist Richard Thaler Wins Nobel Prize,' BBC, October 9, 2017.

30 *Another way of nudging people*
'Volkswagen Sweden "The Fun Theory" by DDB Stockholm,' *Campaign*, October 14, 2009.

30   They decided to nudge commuters
Theaker A, '*The Public Relations Handbook,*' Routledge, 2013.

30   Stairs at a Stockholm metro station
DemonTaste, 'Piano Stairs – Odenplan, Stockholm, Sweden,' YouTube, August 24, 2012.

31   A transparent bin outside a London tube station
'Reducing Cigarette Butt Litter,' Local Government Association, UK, May 20, 2018.
https://www.local.gov.uk/case-studies/reducing-cigarette-butt-litter
(Accessed: July 12, 2022).

31   Purists might argue that adding an incentive
Hansen PG, 'The Definition of Nudge and Libertarian Paternalism: Does the Hand Fit the Glove?' *European Journal of Risk Regulation* 7(1), 2016, 155-174.
'Nudge, Fun Theory & the Role of Incentives in Libertarian Paternalism,' February 20, 2012.
https://inudgeyou.com/en/nudge-fun-theory-the-role-of-incentives-in-libertarian-paternalism/
(Accessed: July 12, 2022).

32   Instead of telling veterans that they were eligible
'The Power of Nudges: Maya Shankar on Changing People's Minds,' Knowledge at Wharton, June 1, 2021.
Shankar M, 'Why We Do What We Do,' End Well Symposium, December 6, 2018.

32   Every year, the state spent 20 million dollars
Nodjimbadem, K, 'The Trashy Beginnings of 'Don't Mess with Texas',' *Smithsonian Magazine*, March 10, 2017.

32   Their slogan, 'Don't Mess with Texas'
Houston Press, 'Dallas Cowboys Say, "Don't Mess with Texas",' YouTube, January 11, 2011.

32   In the first six years of the campaign
Kiscaden R, 'Behaviour Change Can Be Difficult – Use the "Nudge" for Real Results,' *Energy Central*, August 21, 2018.

32   In 2014, about 550 million people
Anecdotes on Swachh Bharat Mission (SBM) are from the following sources:
Dinnoo S, 'Why Do Millions of Indians Defecate in the Open?' BBC, June 17, 2014.
Chengappa R, 'The Swachh Yogi,' *India Today*, December 30, 2019.
Bicchieri C, Mcnally P, Ghai S, and Patel R, 'How Trendsetters Shaped India's Massive Sanitation Campaign,' Knowledge at Wharton, September 20, 2019.

34   *This framework, known by its acronym EAST*
'EAST: Four Simple Ways to Apply Behavioural Insights,' The Behavioural Insights Team, 2014.
https://www.bi.team/publications/east-four-simple-ways-to-apply-behavioural-insights/
(Accessed: July 12, 2022).

35   *The movie reinforced and spread a message*
Iyer P, *'The Swachh Bharat Revolution: Four Pillars of India's Behavioural Transformation,'* Harper Collins India, 2019.
Singh SN, director, *'Toilet: Ek Prem Katha* (translated Toilet: A Love Story),' Viacom 18 Motion Pictures, August 2017.

35   *Swachh Bharat Mission has, perhaps*
Iyer P, 'How the Swachh Bharat Mission Is Nudging People to Use Toilets,' *Hindustan Times*, January 25, 2019.

36   *Germany has an opt-in policy*
Johnson EJ and Goldstein D, 'Do Defaults Save Lives?,' *Science* 302(5649), 2003, 1338-1339.

37   *Can a cup of hot tea or coffee*
Williams LE and Bargh JA, 'Experiencing Physical Warmth Promotes Interpersonal Warmth,' *Science* 322(5901), 2008, 606-607.
Dillon R, Sperling J, and Tietz J, 'A Small Nudge to Create Stunning Team Results,' McKinsey & Company, October 29, 2018.

38   *This is also called the Hawthorne Effect*
Mayo E, Roethlisberger FJ, and Dickson WJ, 'The Human Relations Movement: Harvard Business School and the Hawthorne Experiments (1924-1933)', 2009.
https://www.library.hbs.edu/hc/hawthorne/intro.html
(Accessed: July 12, 2022).
Levitt, SD and List JA, 'Was There Really a Hawthorne Effect at the Hawthorne Plant? An Analysis of the Original Illumination Experiments,' *American Economic Journal: Applied Economics* 3(1), 2011, 224-38.

38   *Over an eight-month period, the airline*
Lambert C, Harvey E, Kinstruck D, Gosnell G, List J, and Metcalfe R, 'The Effects of Giving Captains Feedback and Targets on SOP Fuel and Carbon Efficiency Information,' Virgin Atlantic, University of Chicago and The London School of Economics, 2016.
Gosnell GK, John AL, and Robert DM, 'The Impact of Management Practices on Employee Productivity: A Field Experiment with Airline Captains,' *Journal of Political Economy* 128(4), 2020, 1195-1233.

39   *Notifying captains [pilots] that fuel*
Holder M, 'Could a Change in Pilot Behaviour Save Airlines Carbon and Costs?' *Business Green*, June 27, 2016.

Lambert C, Harvey E, Kinstruck D, Gosnell G, List J, and Metcalfe R, 'The Effects of Giving Captains Feedback and Targets on SOP Fuel and Carbon Efficiency Information,' Virgin Atlantic, University of Chicago and The London School of Economics, 2016.

39   Recognizing his vulnerability, Odysseus
Sally D, 'I, Too, Sail Past: Odysseus and the Logic of Self-Control,' *Kyklos* 53(2), 2000, 173-200.
Nussbaum D, 'Odysseus Nudged: How Limiting our Choices Can Give Us More Freedom,' *Big Think*, May 24, 2013.

40   According to Dan Ariely, a professor
Ariely D, '*Predictably Irrational: The Hidden Forces That Shape Our Decisions,*' Harper Collins, 2010.

41   When it is accessible and displayed prominently
Hanks AS, Just DR, Smith LE, and Wansink B, 'Healthy Convenience: Nudging Students toward Healthier Choices in the Lunchroom,' *Journal of Public Health* 34(3), 2012, 370-376.
Leonard TC, Thaler RH, and Sunstein CR, 'Nudge: Improving Decisions about Health, Wealth, and Happiness,' *Constitutional Political Economy* 19(4), 2008, 356–360.
Rozin P, Scott S, Dingley M, Urbanek JK, Jiang H, and Kaltenbach M, 'Nudge to Nobesity I: Minor Changes in Accessibility Decrease Food Intake,' *Judgment and Decision Making* 6(4), 2011, 323-332.

42   A cafeteria at Google has this sign
Chance Z, Dhar R, Hatzis M, and Bakker M, 'How Google Optimized Healthy Office Snacks,' *Harvard Business Review*, 2016, 2-6.
https://hbr.org/2016/03/how-google-uses-behavioral-economics-to-make-its-employees-healthier
(Accessed: August 12, 2022).

42   Dan, the psychology professor from earlier
Ariely D and Wertenbroch K, 'Procrastination, Deadlines, and Performance: Self-Control by Precommitment,' *Psychological Science* 13(3), 2002, 219-224.

44   Mathematician and meteorologist Edward Lorenz
Lorenz E and R Abraham (Eds.), 'The Chaos Avant-Garde Memories of the Early Days of Chaos Theory,' World Scientific Series on Nonlinear Science Series, 2000, 91-94.

44   A friend called it 'Does the flap of a butterfly's wings
Lorenz E, 'Predictability: Does the Flap of a Butterfly's Wing in Brazil Set Off a Tornado in Texas?' American Association for the Advancement of Science, December 29, 1972.
https://eapsweb.mit.edu/sites/default/files/Butterfly_1972.pdf
(Accessed: July 27, 2022).

44   *As a graduate student, Brad Myers*
Myers BA, 'The Importance of Percent-Done Progress Indicators for Computer-Human Interfaces,' *ACM SIGCHI Bulletin* 16(4), 1985, 11-17.

44   *In some cases, performances may also*
Ariely D, Uri G, George L, and Nina M, 'Large Stakes and Big Mistakes,' *The Review of Economic Studies* 76 (2), 2009, 451-469.

45   *Alcoholics Anonymous doesn't expect its members*
Weick KE, 'Small Wins: Redefining the Scale of Social Problems,' *American Psychologist* 39(1), 1984, 40–49.

45   *Teresa Amabile is a professor at Harvard*
Amabile T and Kramer S, *'The Progress Principle: Using Small Wins to Ignite Joy, Engagement, and Creativity at Work,'* Harvard Business Press, 2011.

46   *I smashed that bug that's been frustrating me*
Ibid.

46   *In 1968, Frederick Herzberg*
Herzberg F, 'One More Time: How Do You Motivate Employees?' *Harvard Business Review* 81(1),1968, 53-62.

47   *Behaviour can travel like a contagion*
Anecdotes on social groups are from the following sources:
Christakis NA and Fowler JH, 'Social Contagion Theory: Examining Dynamic Social Networks and Human Behaviour,' *Statistics in Medicine* 32(4), 2013, 556-577.
Christakis NA and Fowler JH, 'The Spread of Obesity in a Large Social Network over 32 years,' *New England Journal of Medicine* 357(4), 2007, 370-379.
Christakis NA and Fowler JH, 'The Collective Dynamics of Smoking in a Large Social Network,' *New England Journal of Medicine* 358(21), 2008, 2249-2258.
Fowler JH and Christakis NA, 'Dynamic Spread of Happiness in a Large Social Network: Longitudinal Analysis over 20 Years in the Framingham Heart Study,' *British Medical Journal*, 2008, 337-338.
Stossel S, 'You and Your Friend's Friends,' *New York Times*, October 1, 2009.

48   *How we feel, what we know*
Christakis NA and Fowler JH, *'Connected: The Amazing Power of Social Networks and How They Shape Our Lives,'* Harper Collins, 2010.

48   *If you are waiting for a pay hike*
Ibid.

48   *The United Nations estimates that the death toll*
Friedman EA, 'Behind the Headlines: 10 Million Deaths from Antimicrobial Resistance by 2050 (or Not?),' O'Neill Institute for National & Global Health Law, December 2, 2020.

https://oneill.law.georgetown.edu/behind-the-headlines-10-million-antimicrobial-deaths-by-2050-or-not/
(Accessed: July 27, 2022).

Interagency Coordination Group on Antimicrobial Resistance, 'No Time to Wait: Securing the Future from Drug-Resistant Infections Report to the Secretary-General of the United Nations,' April 2019.
https://www.who.int/docs/default-source/documents/no-time-to-wait-securing-the-future-from-drug-resistant-infections-en.pdf
(Accessed: July 27, 2022).

49   *The chief medical officer in England*
Hallsworth M, Chadborn T, Sallis A, Sanders M, Berry D, Greaves F, Clements L, and Davies SC, 'Provision of Social Norm Feedback to High Prescribers of Antibiotics in General Practice: A Pragmatic National Randomised Controlled Trial,' *The Lancet* 387(10029), 2016, 1743-1752.

49   *Scott Stevens had a master's degree*
Rosengren J, 'How Casinos Enable Gambling Addicts,' *The Atlantic*, December 2016.

50   *When someone wins, the jingles*
Research on the dark side of gambling is from the following sources:
Dixon MJ, Harrigan KA, Santesso DL, Graydon C, Fugelsang JA, and Collins K, 'The Impact of Sound in Modern Multiline Video Slot Machine Play,' *Journal of Gambling Studies* 30(4), 2014, 913-929.
Clark L, Crooks B, Clarke R, Aitken MRF, and Dunn BD, 'Physiological Responses to Near-Miss Outcomes and Personal Control During Simulated Gambling,' *Journal of Gambling Studies* 28(1), 2012, 123-137.
Dixon MJ and Daar J, 'Losses Disguised as Wins, the Science Behind Casino Profits,' *The Conversation*, November 4, 2014.
Jensen C, Dixon MJ, Harrigan KA, Sheepy E, Fugelsang JA, and Jarick M, 'Misinterpreting "Winning" in Multiline Slot Machine Games,' *International Gambling Studies* 13, 2013,112-126.
Leino T, Torsheim T, Pallesen S, Blaszczynski A, Sagoe D, and Molde H, 'An Empirical Real-World Study of Losses Disguised as Wins in Electronic Gaming Machines,' *International Gambling Studies* 16, 2016, 470-480.

51   *Gamblers often believe that they win*
Dixon MR and Schreiber JE, 'Near-Miss Effects on Response Latencies and Win Estimations of Slot Machine Players,' *The Psychological Record* 54(3), 2004, 335-348.

51   *Stacy's legal counsel argued*
Rosengren J, 'How Casinos Enable Gambling Addicts,' *The Atlantic*, December 2016.

51   *Thaler, the Nobel Prize winning economist*
Thaler R, 'The Power of Nudges, for Good and Bad,' *New York Times*, October 31, 2015.

Chapter 3 – Be Intellectually Humble

56   ***The interviewer asks***
      Anecdotes on interviewing at Google are from the following sources:
      Carlson N, '15 Google Interview Questions That Will Make You Feel Stupid,'
      Insider, November 8, 2010.
      Fried I, 'Google Received 3.3 Million Job Applications in 2019,' *Axios*, January
      9, 2020.
      Shontell A, 'Google Admits Its Crazy Interview Questions Were "A Complete
      Waste of Time",' Insider, June 20, 2013.
      Friedman TL, 'How to Get a Job at Google,' *New York Times*, February 22,
      2014.

56   ***Getting a job at Google is tougher***
      Lake S, 'How to Get into Harvard Business School,' *Fortune*, April 28, 2021.

57   ***Illustration: Recruitment at Google***
      Adapted from: Salerno R, 'The Good, the Good and the Good about Working
      at Google,' August 7, 2014.
      https://www.smartrecruiters.com/blog/google-averages-130-applicants-to-
      make-one-hire/
      (Accessed: July 12, 2022).

58   ***Without intellectual humility***
      Bock L, *'Work Rules: Insights from Inside Google That Will Transform How You
      Live and Lead,'* John Murray, 2015.

59   ***Which of these statements***
      Leary MR, Diebels KJ, Davisson EK, Jongman-Sereno KP, Isherwood JC,
      Raimi KT, Deffler SA, and Hoyle RH, 'Cognitive and Interpersonal Features
      of Intellectual Humility,' *Personality and Social Psychology Bulletin* 43(6), 2017,
      793-813.

59   ***Much of our understanding of mindsets***
      Discussion on mindset is from the following sources:
      Dweck CS, *'Mindset: The New Psychology of Success,'* Penguin Random House,
      2006.
      Dweck C, 'What Having a Growth Mindset Actually Means,' *Harvard Business
      Review*, January 2016, 2-4.
      https://hbr.org/2016/01/what-having-a-growth-mindset-actually-means
      (Accessed: August 12, 2022).
      Dweck CS and Yeager DS, 'Mindsets: A View from Two Eras,' *Perspectives on
      Psychological Science: A Journal of the Association for Psychological Science* 14(3),
      2019, 481-496.
      Hong Y, Chiu C, Dweck CS, Lin DMS, and Wan W, 'Implicit Theories,
      Attributions, and Coping: A Meaning System Approach,' *Journal of Personality
      and Social Psychology* 77(3), 1999, 588-599.

'Intelligence: Is It Fixed? Carol Dweck and the Growth Mindset,' Montrose42 Blog, August 24, 2013.
https://montrose42.wordpress.com/2013/08/24/intelligence-is-it-fixed-carol-dweck-and-the-growth-mindset/
(Accessed: July 12, 2022).

60   Recruiters at Google look for 'Googleyness'
Holly F, 'Missions that Matter,' *Think with Google*, July 2011.
https://www.thinkwithgoogle.com/future-of-marketing/emerging-technology/missions-that-matter/
(Accessed: July 12, 2022.

60   Attributes like fun
Bock L, '*Work Rules: Insights from Inside Google That Will Transform How You Live and Lead,*' John Murray, 2015.

60   The University of Hongkong (HKU)
Prince S, 'There's Good Reason HKU Is the Harvard of the East,' *South China Morning Post*, May 15, 2014.

61   Students who hold a fixed view
Dweck CS, '*Mindset: The New Psychology of Success,*' Penguin Random House, 2006.

62   I have missed more than 9,000 shots
Jordan M, Forbes Quotes: Thoughts on the Business of Life, n.d.
https://www.forbes.com/quotes/11194/
(Accessed: 25 May 2022).

63   Melanie Stefan also remembers that year
Stefan M, 'A CV of Failures,' *Nature* 468(7322), 2010, 467.

63   Cool, I am like Ronaldinho
Herrera T, 'Do You Keep a Failure Résumé? Here's Why You Should Start,' *New York Times*, February 3, 2019.

63   Even his exclusion from the World Cup squad
'Why Was Ronaldinho Not Called Up for FIFA World Cup,' Quora, n.d.
https://www.quora.com/Why-was-Ronaldinho-not-called-up-for-FIFA-World-Cup-2010
(Accessed: January 20, 2022).

63   Didn't make it, not even close
Warikoo A, 'My Failure Resume,' YouTube, November 23, 2021.

64   Illustration: This is Ankur's failure resume
Warikoo A, 'My Failure Resume,' 2016.
https://www.ankurwarikoo.com/wp-content/uploads/2016/06/Ankur-Warikoo-Failure-Resume-1.pdf
(Accessed: July 31, 2022).

65   *We broke down too*
Warikoo A, *'Do Epic Shit,'* Juggernaut, 2022.

65   *I had no money, no plan, no direction*
Warikoo A, 'My Failure Resume,' YouTube, November 23, 2021.

66   *Ankur is now a blogger on social media*
Kuenzang K, 'HT Brunch Cover Story: Viral and Unpredictable,' *Hindustan Times*, December 28, 2021.

67   *At least that's what Dana Carney*
Anecdotes on Dana Carney and Amy Cuddy are from the following sources:
Carney DR, Cuddy AJC, and Yap AJ, 'Power Posing: Brief Nonverbal Displays Affect Neuroendocrine Levels and Risk Tolerance,' *Psychological Science* 21(10), 2010, 1363-1368.
Cuddy, A, 'TED: Your Body Language May Shape Who You Are,' YouTube, October 1, 2012.
Cuddy A, *'Presence: Bringing Your Boldest Self to Your Biggest Challenges,'* Little, Brown Spark, 2015.

68   *Many social scientists have even discredited*
Engber D, 'Did Power-Posing Guru Amy Cuddy Deserve Her Public Shaming?' *Slate*, October 19, 2017.
Bartlett T, 'Power Poser: When Big Ideas Go Bad,' *The Chronicle of Higher Education* 63(16), 2016,
Elsesser K, 'The Debate on Power Posing Continues: Here's Where We Stand,' *Forbes*, October 2, 2020.

68   *As evidence has come in over these past 2+ years*
Carney DR, 'My Position on "Power Poses,"' Unpublished Manuscript, University of California, 2016.
https://faculty.haas.berkeley.edu/dana_carney/pdf_my%20position%20on%20power%20poses.pdf
(Accessed: August 10, 2022).

68   *Since then, she has worked on studies*
Jonas, KJ, Cesario J, Alger M, Bailey AH, Bombari D, Carney D, et al., 'Power Poses – Where Do We Stand?' *Comprehensive Results in Social Psychology* 2(1), 2017, 139-141.

68   *In contrast, Amy, who was the second author*
Cuddy, A, *'Presence: Bringing Your Boldest Self to Your Biggest Challenges,'* Little, Brown Spark, 2015.

68   *She stopped taking calls*
Dominus S, 'When the Revolution Came for Amy Cuddy,' *New York Times*, October 18, 2017.

69   ***They found that 33 per cent of the studies***
Camerer CF, Dreber A, Holzmeister F, Ho T, Huber J, Johannesson, et al., 'Evaluating the Replicability of Social Science Experiments in Nature and Science between 2010 and 2015,' *Nature Human Behaviour* 2(9), 2018, 637-644.

69   ***This upheaval led to a 'Loss of Confidence Project'***
Rohrer JM, Tierney W, Uhlmann EL, DeBruine LM, Heyman T, Jones BC, et al., 'Putting the Self in Self-Correction: Findings from the Loss-of-Confidence Project,' *Perspectives on Psychological Science* 16(6), 2021, 1255-1269.

69   ***For Laszlo, the head of Google's People Operations***
Friedman TL, 'How to Get a Job at Google,' *New York Times*, February 22, 2014.

69   ***[Successful people will] be zealots***
Ibid.

69   ***They are debating the existence of God***
Sprouts, 'The Confirmation Bias,' YouTube, December 31, 2019.

71   ***Valdis Krebs, a network researcher, mapped***
Krebs V, 'Working in the Connected World,' *IHRIM Journal* 4(2), 2000, 89-91.

71   ***Neuroscientists tell us that***
Kaplan JT, Gimbel SI, and Harris S, 'Neural Correlates of Maintaining One's Political Beliefs in the Face of Counterevidence,' *Scientific Reports* 6(39589), 2016, 1-11.

72   ***Alice Stewart, an epidemiologist and physician***
The anecdote on Alice and George is from the following sources:
Ranadive A, 'Why It's Important to "Dare to Disagree",' *Medium*, June 2, 2017.
Heffernan M, 'TED: Dare to Disagree,' YouTube, August 6, 2012.
Cantor D, 'Gayle Greene, the Woman Who Knew Too Much: Alice Stewart and the Secrets of Radiation,' Ann Arbor, University of Michigan Press, 1999.

73   ***It takes more than 20 years***
Stewart A, 'Women in World History,' A Biographical Encyclopaedia.
https://www.encyclopedia.com/women/encyclopedias-almanacs-transcripts-and-maps/stewart-alice-1906
(Accessed: June 1, 2022).

74   ***In 1995, McArthur Wheeler***
Weintraub P, 'What Know-It-All Don't Know, or the Illusion of Competence,' *Aeon Ideas*, December 17, 2016.
https://aeon.co/ideas/what-know-it-alls-dont-know-or-the-illusion-of-competence
(Accessed: July 12, 2022).

74 **But I wore the juice**
Fehlhaber K, 'Why a Bank Robber Thought Covering Himself in Lemon Juice Would Help Him Get Away with It,' *Quartz*, May 19, 2017.

75 **Along with his student Justin Kruger**
Kruger J and Dunning D, 'Unskilled and Unaware of It: How Difficulties in Recognizing One's Own Incompetence Lead to Inflated Self-Assessments,' *Journal of Personality and Social Psychology* 77(6), 2000, 1121-1134.

75 **Incompetence does not leave people disoriented**
Dunning D, 'We Are All Confident Idiots,' *Pacific Standard*, October 27, 2014.

75 **A toilet test tried to prove**
Rozenblit L and Keil F, 'The Misunderstood Limits of Folk Science: An Illusion of Explanatory Depth,' *Cognitive Science* 26(5), 2002, 521-562.

76 **Illustration: Dunning Kruger Effect**
Adapted from:
https://fourweekmba.com/dunning-kruger-effect/
(Accessed: April 12, 2022).

76 **People who are right a lot, listen a lot**
Bariso J, 'Jeff Bezos's Viral Tweet Is Only 38 Words, but It Teaches a Master Class in How to Handle Criticism,' *Inc*, October 2021.

77 **Fortunately, that year, Babson College**
Reynolds PD, Bygrave WD, Autio E, Cox LW, and Hay M, 'Global Entrepreneurship Monitor, 2002 Executive Report,' Babson College, Ewing Marion Kauffman Foundation, London Business School, 2002.

Chapter 4 – Dance with Disciplines

82 **Andre Geim, a physicist, won an Ig Nobel Prize**
Ashton J, 'Sir Andre Geim Interview: Father of Graphene – I'm an Alien among My Own, and on My Own Among Aliens,' *The Independent*, November 10, 2014.

82 **When a frog, whose body is 75 per cent water**
Tracy DA, 'Where Have All the Frogs Gone,' Michigan State University Extension, March 4, 2015.

82 **Don't worry, our smiling frog was not harmed**
Science News Staff, 'Floating Frogs,' April 14, 1997.
https://www.science.org/content/article/floating-frogs
(Accessed: August 3, 2022).

82 **The head of a religious group**
Charles D, 'Ig Nobel to Nobel: Creative (and Fun) Science Wins,' NPR, October 5, 2010.

82   *In 2011, a Japanese team invented*

Reuters Life, 'Wasabi Fire Alarm a Lifesaver for the Deaf,' Reuters, March 18, 2008.

Jha A, 'Wasabi Fire Alarm Scoops Ig Nobel Prize for Japanese Scientists,' *The Guardian*, September 30, 2011.

82   *Researchers at the National Institute of Mental*

Balasubramanian D, 'The Nobel and the Ig Nobel Prizes,' *The Hindu*, November 4, 2017.

Abrahams M, 'Why Teenagers Get Right Up Your Nose,' *The Guardian*, August 19, 2008.

83   *In 2002, mathematicians from the College of Veterinary*

Pulla P, 'Ig Nobel Indians,' *The Open Magazine*, April 1, 2012.

83   *The Ig Nobel award ceremony is held at Harvard*

The Ig Nobel Prizes were instituted by Marc Abrahams, Science Humour Magazine.

'About Marc Abrahams,' Improbable Research, n.d.
https://improbable.com/about/people/MarcAbrahams.html
(Accessed: February 11, 2022).

'Ig Nobel Prize,' Google Arts and Culture,' n.d. https://artsandculture.google.com/entity/ig-nobel-prize/m03xt2?hl=en
(Accessed: February 11, 2022).

83   *I do not dig deep, I graze shallow*

Geim A, 'U. Manchester's Andre Geim: Sticking with Graphene – for now,' *Science Watch*, August 2008.

83   *With his colleagues, Andre invented gecko tape*

Knight W, 'Gecko Tape Will Stick You to Ceiling,' *New Scientist*, June 1, 2003.
https://www.newscientist.com/article/dn3785-gecko-tape-will-stick-you-to-ceiling/
(Accessed: August 11, 2022).

84   *Thomson-Reuters named Andre*

'Graphene and 2D Virtual Conference and Expo,' *Graphene Online*, 2020.
http://grapheneconf.archivephantomsnet.net/2020/speakersinfo.php
(Accessed: January 31, 2022).

84   *For his work on graphene*

'The Nobel Prize in Physics 2010,' The Nobel Prize, 2010.
https://www.nobelprize.org/prizes/physics/2010/summary/
(Accessed: June 12, 2022).

85   *Manjul had a very intuitive way of solving them*

Anecdotes on Manjul Bharagava are from the following sources:
Schultz S, 'Bhargava Strikes Balance among Many Interests,' *Princeton Weekly Bulletin* 93(12), 2003.

Mehta N, 'Indian-Origin Mathematician Manjul Bhargava Wins Fields Medal,' *Mint.* August 13, 2014.

Bhargava M, 'Higher Composition Laws and Applications,' International Congress of Mathematicians 2, 2007, 271-294.

86   *Mathematics is very much a playful experience*

Klarreich E, 'The Musical, Magical Number Theorist,' *Quanta Magazine*, August 12, 2014.

Quanta, 'Manjul Bhargava: The Musical, Magical Number Theorist,' YouTube, June 15, 2015.

86   *They both co-taught 'Introduction to Music'*

Gallian JA, 'Manjul Bhargava: Budding Superstar,' *Math Horizons* 14(1), 2006, 16-17.

87   *Suppose you have 8 beats*

Krishnamachari S, 'The Musical Formula,' *The Hindu*, January 14, 2016.

NDTV, 'Poetry, Daisies and Cobras: Math Class with Manjul Bhargava,' YouTube, Mar 8, 2015.

87   *It is also known as the Fibonacci sequence*

'Fibonacci Sequence,' Encyclopaedia Britannica, March 14, 2022.
https://www.britannica.com/science/Fibonacci-number
(Accessed: June 12, 2022).

88   *He offers a freshman course*

Kelly M, 'In the Art of Mathematics, Work Is Play and Tricks Are the Trade,' Office of Communications, Princeton University, March 25, 2013.

88   *Most of us have tunnel vision*

Pittman P, 'Chris Anderson Is the Curator of TED,' *Dumbo Feather*, July 1, 2011.

88   *A conference on technology, entertainment, and design*

'TED History of TED: How Did a One-Off Conference about Technology, Entertainment and Design Become a Viral Video Phenomenon and a Worldwide Community of Passionate People?'
https://www.ted.com/about/our-organization/history-of-ted
(Accessed: June 12, 2022).

88   *It is called the Annual Ted Conference*

Ellis EG, 'The Oral History of TED, a Club for the Rich that Became a Global Phenomenon,' *Wired*, April 20, 2017.

89   *Till the eighth grade, Chris attended Woodstock School*

Ghosh A, 'Changing the World, One Thought at a Time,' *Hindustan Times*, November 11, 2017.

'Chris Anderson 1974,' Woodstock School.
https://www.woodstockschool.in/alumni/distinguished-alumni/anderson/
(Accessed: February 1, 2022).

89 *Many videos have been viewed over a billion times*
'TED Talks,' TED, 2019.
https://www.ted.com/about/programs-initiatives/ted-talks
(Accessed: February 11, 2022).

90 *We think visually, we think in sound*
Robinson SK, 'Do Schools Kill Creativity?' TED, January 7, 2007.

90 *You need to understand how human beings*
Geere D, 'Matt Ridley Observes "Ideas Having Sex,"' *Wired,* July 21, 2010.
Ridley M, 'TED: When Ideas Have Sex,' YouTube, July 19, 2010.
Ridley M, *'How Innovation Works and Why It Flourishes in Freedom,'* Harper, 2020.

90 *Foraging tools were used*
Diamond JM, 'The Tasmanians: The Longest Isolation, the Simplest Technology,' *Nature* 273(5659), 1978, 185-186.

90 *For instance, Hawaii with a population of 275,000*
Kline MA and Boyd R, 'Population Size Predicts Technological Complexity in Oceania,' Proceedings of the Royal Society B: *Biological Sciences* 277(1693), 2010, 2559-2564.
Ridley M, 'Why Some Islanders Build Better Crab Traps,' *Wall Street Journal,* October 2, 2010.

91 *The Renaissance, with its sociocultural transitions*
Burckhardt J, *'The Civilization of the Renaissance in Italy,'* Translated by S Middlemore, Penguin Classics, 1860/1990.

92 *Europe, in this era, became a hotbed*
Johansson F, *'The Medici Effect: Breakthrough Insights at the Intersection of Ideas, Concepts, and Cultures,'* Harvard Business School Press, 2004.

92 *While describing his field, Freeman Dyson*
Dyson F, 'Birds and Frogs,' Notices of the American Mathematical Society (AMS) 56(2), 2009, 212-223.

93 *It is a problem with interdependencies*
Cheung J, 'Applying Design Thinking to Wicked Problems,' *Career Foundry,* June 10, 2022.
https://careerfoundry.com/en/blog/ux-design/wicked-problems/
(Accessed: August 1, 2022).

93 *There are wicked problems at the workplace as well*
Camillus JC, 'Strategy as a Wicked Problem,' *Harvard Business Review* 86(5), 2008, 98-101.

94 *Illustration: I- and T-shaped profiles*
Adapted from: Yip J, 'Why T-Shaped People?' *Medium,* March 24, 2018.

94   IDEO, a design and consulting firm
IDEO means 'idea' in Greek. The company was formed by the merger of
David Kelly Design, Stanford University, and Moggridge Associates, London
in 1991.
'International Directory of Company Histories: IDEO Inc.,' Encyclopedia.com,
2003.

94   The best leaders will integrate emerging new disciplines
Anecdotes on IDEO are from the following sources:
Buell RW and Otazo A, 'IDEO: Human Centered Design,' *Harvard Business
School Case*, 9-615-022, 2016, 1-20.
Thomke AS and Nimgade A, 'IDEO Product Development,' *Harvard Business
School Case*, 9-680-143, 2017, 1-21.
Neri A, 'ABC Nightline – IDEO Shopping Cart,' YouTube, December 3, 2009.

95   Experts of all flavours co-mingle
'IDEO', HR Magazine, June 1, 2001.
https://www.hrmagazine.co.uk/content/features/ideo
(Accessed: August 1, 2022).

95   A liberal education does not teach
Zakaria F, '*In Defence of a Liberal Education*,' W. W. Norton & Company, 2016.

96   Yale University is known for its liberal arts curriculum
https://admissions.yale.edu/liberal-arts-education
(Accessed: February 11, 2022).

96   'The Future of Jobs', a report
Schwab K and Samans R, 'The Future of Jobs Report,' World Economic Forum,
2016.

97   It is the way you are taught
Pramath Sinha's quotes are from his interactions and talks at Ashoka University
on various occasions.
https://www.ashoka.edu.in/profile/pramath-raj-sinha/
(Accessed: July 11, 2022).

97   I learned about serifs and sans-serif typefaces
Garfield S, 'One Thing We Owe to Steve Jobs,' CNN, October 6, 2011.

97   At 17, Robert had joined the Trappist Order
Fox M, 'Rev. Robert Palladino, Scribe Who Shaped Apple's Fonts, Dies at 83,'
New York Times, March 4, 2016.

98   In the American comedy-drama film Liberal Arts
Radnor J, director, '*Liberal Arts*,' Strategic Motion Ventures, 2012.

98   I was English (sic)
Ibid.

99 *What can't be replaced in any organization*
Perrault T, 'Digital Companies Need More Liberal Arts Majors,' *Harvard Business Review*, January 29, 2016.
https://hbr.org/2016/01/digital-companies-need-more-liberal-arts-majors
(Accessed: August 11, 2022).

100 *Curiosity, in fact, helps children think critically*
Stumm SV, Hell B. and Chamorro-Premuzic T, 'The Hungry Mind: Intellectual Curiosity Is the Third Pillar of Academic Performance,' *Perspectives on Psychological Science* 6(6), 2011, 574-588.

100 *A desire for knowledge can motivate*
Hardy III JH, Ness AM, and Mecca J, 'Outside the Box: Epistemic Curiosity as a Predictor of Creative Problem Solving and Creative Performance,' *Personality and Individual Differences* 104, 2017, 230-237.

100 *We are entering into someone else's territory*
Lewis S, 'The Deliberate Amateur,' *Slate*, May 21, 2014.

101 *Edward de Bono, author of Six Thinking Hats*
De Bono E, '*Six Thinking Hats: An Essential Approach to Business Management,*' Penguin Random House, 1999.

101 *Too much experience within a field*
De Bono E, '*Practical Thinking: Four Ways to Be Right, Five Ways to Be Wrong,*' Penguin Random House, 2017.

101 *Saikat Majumdar, our colleague at Ashoka*
Majumdar S, '*College: Pathways of Possibility,*' Bloomsbury Publishing, 2018.

102 *The future of computer science is the intersection*
Shankar A, 'Bigger Campus, More Student Intake: Ashoka University's Expansion Plan,' *Indian Express*, May 16, 2022.
https://indianexpress.com/article/cities/delhi/bigger-campus-more-student-intake-ashoka-universitys-expansion-plan-7919086/
(Accessed: August 11, 2022).

102 *At first glance, digital humanities*
Purayil SP, 'Digital Humanities in India,' The Centre for Internet and Society, November 12, 2014.
Kaylaw, 'Digital Humanities: An Oxymoron?' Transnational Theory and Criticism, The University of Maryland, December 4, 2014.

103 *You are now an employee of the British*
Anecdotes on Bletchley Park and Alan Turing are from the following sources:
Hill M, '*Bletchley Park People: Churchill's Geese that Never Cackled,*' Sutton Publishing, 2004.
Cowell A, 'Overlooked No More: Alan Turing, Condemned Code Breaker and Computer Visionary,' *New York Times*, June 5, 2019.

Cambridge University, 'Alan Turing – Celebrating the Life of a Genius,' YouTube, June 21, 2012.

Dockterman E, 'The True Story of "The Imitation Game",' *Time*, November 28, 2014.

Bailin A and Halford J, 'Alan Turing Pardon: We Need a Shift in Legal Position,' *The Guardian*, December 19, 2012.

103 ***Do not talk at meals***
Budiansky S, *'Battle of Wits: The Complete Story of Codebreaking in World War II,'* Simon and Schuster, 2002.

104 ***Illustration: The Daily Telegraph Crossword***
Turing A, 'The Puzzle Before Bletchley Park,' *New York Times*. January 13, 1942.
https://www.nytimes.com/crosswords/game/paid/alan-turing
(Accessed: July 11, 2022).

106 ***He described the Bletchley Park codebreakers***
Hill M, *'Bletchley Park People: Churchill's Geese that Never Cackled,'* Sutton Publishing, 2004.

106 ***His life has been poignantly captured***
Tyldum M, director, '*The Imitation Game*,' Black Bear Pictures, 2014.

106 ***The Turing Award, named after him***
Copeland J, 'Alan Turing: The Codebreaker Who Saved "Millions of Lives,"' BBC News, June 19, 2012.
Hosch WL, 'Turing Award: Computer Science Award,' Britannica, 2009/2022.

106 ***A human being should be able to***
Hansen D, 'Do Businesses Need More Generalists?' *Forbes,* December 22, 2012.

Chapter 5 – Curate the Chaos

110 ***The fact that you are still working for me***
Szramiak J, 'This Story about Warren Buffett and His Long-Time Pilot Is an Important Lesson about What Separates Extraordinarily Successful People from Everyone Else,' *Business Insider*, December 4, 2017.

111 ***Tuma's playlist, 'RapCaviar', has 14 million***
SoundLog (@soundloghq), 'With Almost 14 Million Followers Rap Caviar Is the Premier Hip Hop Playlist on Spotify,' Twitter, May 3, 2021.
https://twitter.com/soundloghq/status/1389234143997792257
(Accessed: June 1, 2022).

111 ***I am not a creator, I am a curator***
Revolt, '#IAmRevolt – Tuma Basa (VP Of Music Programming),' YouTube, August 2013.

112   Rohit Bhargava, an adjunct professor
Bhargava R, 'Non-Obvious: How to Think Different, Curate Ideas & Predict the Future,' Idea Press Publishing, 2017.

112   Illustration: Manifesto-Job Description
Ibid.

113   As a 25-year-old, DeWitt Wallace
Ferguson C, 'Unforgettable Dewitt Wallace,' Reader's Digest, February 14, 2022.

113   Initially published from the basement
As on March 2022, Reader's Digest had 100 million readers worldwide. It is the largest selling magazine in the world, published in 48 editions and 19 languages, and sold in more than 60 countries.
'Reader's Digest, World's Most Widely Read Magazine,' India Today Group, n.d.
https://www.indiatodaygroup.com/new-site/publications/rd-about.html
(Accessed: March 29, 2022).

115   Sheena Iyengar, a professor of business
Anecdotes on narrowing choices are from the following sources:
Iyengar S, 'The Art of Choosing,' Hachette UK, 2010.
Iyengar S and Lepper MR, 'When Choice Is Demotivating: Can One Desire Too Much of a Good Thing?' Journal of Personality and Social Psychology 79(6), 2000, 995-1006.
Iyengar S and Agrawal K, 'Better Choosing Experience,' Strategy & Business 61, 2010, 2-8.

115   I was three when I was diagnosed with retinitis pigmentosa
McHugh F, 'Professor Sheena Iyengar on Choice That Changed Her Life,' South China Morning Post, May 26, 2016.

117   After the purchase, we are also happier
Eisenhardt KM and Sull DN, 'Simple Rules for a Complex World,' Harvard Business Review 90(9), September 2012, 69-74.

117   For managers, simple rules bridge the gap
Sull DN and Eisenhardt KM, 'Simple Rules: How to Thrive in a Complex World,' Houghton Mifflin Harcourt, 2015.

118   Today Sanjiv owns the Zátiší Group
https://www.zatisigroup.cz/en/our-team
(Accessed: March 29, 2022).

118   In Simple Rules, Donald Sull and Kathleen Eisenhardt
Ibid.

119   Netflix realized that using logic
'Lessons from Netflix's Chief Talent Officer,' People Matters, January 10, 2018.

https://www.peoplematters.in/article/leadership/lessons-from-netflixs-chief-talent-officer-17211
(Accessed: August 3, 2022).

119   *Trust people, not policies*
McCord P, 'How Netflix Reinvented HR,' *Harvard Business Review* 92(1-2), 2014, 71-76.

119   *Netflix's expense policy is 'Act in Netflix's best interests'*
'Netflix Culture – Seeking Excellence,' Netflix, n.d.
https://jobs.netflix.com/culture
(Accessed: March 29, 2022).

119   *In 2009, Netflix shared its culture deck*
Zangs E, 'Is Netflix's 2009 Culture Deck Still Relevant Today to Shape Company Culture?' *Forbes*, March 28, 2019.
https://igormroz.com/documents/netflix_culture.pdf
(Accessed: July 11, 2022).

119   *Over the next five years, it was viewed*
McCord P, 'How Netflix Reinvented HR,' *Harvard Business Review* 92(1-2), 2014, 71-76.

119   *Sheryl Sandberg, then COO of Metaverse*
Ferenstein G, 'Read What Facebook's Sandberg Calls Maybe "The Most Important Document Ever to Come Out of the Valley",' *Tech Crunch*, January 31, 2013.

119   *[Just] adequate performance gets*
Greene D, 'Hastings Writes about Netflix's Cultural Reinvention in "No Rules",' NPR Podcast, September 15, 2020.

120   *Strategic fit is a management concept*
Miles S and Clieaf MV, 'Strategic Fit: Key to Growing Enterprise Value through Organizational Capital,' *Harvard Business Review* 60(1), 2017, 55-65.

120   *Las Vegas poker is a game of sharks and fish*
Sull DN and Eisenhardt KM, '*Simple Rules: How to Thrive in a Complex World*,' Houghton Mifflin Harcourt, 2015.

121   *Best known for his books on food*
Pollan M, '*In Defense of Food: An Eater's Manifesto,*' Penguin Random House, 2009.

121   *To eat wisely follow three rules*
Ibid.

121   *Dan Buettner has examined the role that regions*
Buettner D, '*The Blue Zones Kitchen: 100 Recipes to Live to 100,*' National Geographic Books, 2019.

122 *Soft-spoken and petite, Marie*
Kondo M, '*The Life-Changing Magic of Tidying: A Simple, Effective Way to Banish Clutter Forever,*' Penguin Random House, 2014.
'Marie Kondo | The Life-Changing Magic of Tidying Up | Talks at Google,' YouTube, February 25, 2015.

123 *Marie's first book*
Kondo M, '*The Life-Changing Magic of Tidying: A Simple, Effective Way to Banish Clutter Forever,*' Penguin Random House, 2014.

123 *Marie's Netlix show,* **Tidying Up with Marie Kondo**
'Tidying Up with Marie Kondo,' Netflix, September 2, 2017.

124 *I realized my mistake*
Parry RL, 'Marie Kondo Is the Maiden of Mess,' *The Australian*, April 19, 2014.

124 *Sukiyabashi Jiro was the first sushi restaurant*
Shapiro D and Chuck T, 'Obama Begins Asia Trip With "The Best Sushi I've Ever Had",' CNN, April 28, 2014.
Joachim D, 'Obama's First Order of Business in Tokyo: Sushi from the Master,' *New York Times*, April 23, 2014.

124 *Eater Magazine, published by Vox Media*
Tannenbaum K, 'World's Toughest Restaurant Reservations,' *Delish*, February 7, 2012.

125 *All this has been captured by David Gelb*
Rapold N, 'Mastering Fish as an Edible Art Medium,' *New York Times*, March 8, 2012.

125 *This movie is about sushi*
Gelb D, director, '*Jiro Dreams of Sushi,*' Magnolia Pictures, March 2012.

125 *Aware that distractions and interruptions*
Hayward J, 'What Is a Sterile Cockpit and Why Does It Matter?' *Simple Flying*, December 22, 2020.

126 *This rule was enforced after*
Eastern Air Lines Inc, 'Aircraft Accident Report: Eastern Air Lines Inc Douglas DC-9-31, N8984E, Charlotte, North Carolina,' (Report No. NTSB-AAR-75-9), National Transport Safety Board, September 11, 1974.

126 *Momentous Sprint at the 2156 Olympics*
Tatem AJ, Guerra CA, Atkinson PM, and Hay SI, 'Momentous Sprint at the 2156 Olympics?' *Nature* 431(7008), 2004, 525.

126 *It is not logical to say that the first 104 years*
Advanced Placement Biology Class, 'Biology Students Find Holes in Gap Study,' *Nature* 432(7014), 2004, 147.

126   *Another reader wrote a letter*
Ibid.

127   *Carl Bergstrom and Jevin West, both professors*
UW iSchool, 'Calling Bullshit in the Age of Big Data,' YouTube, July 10, 2017.
Bergstrom CT and West J, 'Syllabus: Calling Bullshit – Data Reasoning in a
Digital World' Calling Bullshit, 2019.
https://www.callingbullshit.org/syllabus.html
(Accessed: March 29, 2022).

127   *Ashoka University too offers a similar course*
https://www.ashoka.edu.in/courses-past-philosophy/
(Accessed: June 1, 2022).

127   *In 2008, an article in the medical journal Obesity*
Wang Y, Beydoun MA, Liang L, Caballero B, and Kumanyika SK, 'Will All
Americans Become Overweight or Obese? Estimating the Progression and Cost
of the US Obesity Epidemic,' *Obesity* 16(10), 2008, 2323-2330.

127   *Jorden Elleberg, a researcher, questioned*
Ellenberg J, '*How Not to Be Wrong: The Hidden Maths of Everyday Life*,' Penguin
2014.

128   *Studies show that homicides increase*
Jagannathan M, 'High Temperatures Can Lead to More Violent Crime, Study
Finds,' *New York Post*, June 18, 2019.

128   *Correlation is not causation*
Green N, 'Correlation Is Not Causation,' *The Guardian*, January 6, 2012.

128   *During the pandemic an article*
Giacalone D, Frøst MB, and Rodríguez-Pérez C. 'Reported Changes in Dietary
Habits during the COVID-19 Lockdown in the Danish Population: The Danish
COVID Diet Study,' *Frontiers in Nutrition* 7, 2020, 1-8.
Press Trust of India, 'Drinking Red Wine Can Reduce COVID Risk, Shows
Study. But Here's the Problem,' *Mint*, February 16, 2022.

128   *All this study shows us is that the kind*
Browne E, 'Does Red Wine Prevent COVID? Scientists Question Study
Suggesting It Can,' *Newsweek*, January 27, 2022.

129   *Shekhar Gupta, a news journalist*
'Cut the Clutter,' The Print, n.d.
https://theprint.in/about-us/
(Accessed: March 29, 2022).

129   *If you work hard and intelligently*
Anselment K, '"You're Talking Rot!" Why the Liberal Arts and Sciences Still
Matter,' Lawrence University Blog, February 21, 2013.

129 *I realized the need to present actual research*
'The Story behind Dhruv Rathee,' Nas Academy, n.d.
https://nasacademy.com/blog/article/the-story-behind-dhruv-rathee
(Accessed: July 11, 2022).

130 *Maria was in a class of 400 students*
Schwartz O, 'Maria Popova: Books Are the Original Internet,' *Daily Good*,
February 17, 2019.

130 *This was the beginning of her blog Brain Pickings*
Feiler B, 'She's Got Some Big Ideas,' *New York Times*, November 30, 2012.
Popova, M, 'The Marginalian,' 2006.
https://www.themarginalian.org/
(Accessed: March 29, 2022).

131 *There's information, which is just noise*
Schwartz O, 'Maria Popova: Books Are the Original Internet,' *Daily Good*,
February 17, 2019.

131 *Because of how I've structured my intellectual curiosity*
Levintova H, 'Maria Popova's Beautiful Mind,' *Mother Jones*, January/February
2012.

Chapter 6, Think Entrepreneurially

134 *In 2019, Satvik Hegde was standing*
'World's Most Powerful Selfie Ever: Houston Kid's Click with Trump and Modi
Gets Social Media Talking,' *Financial Express*, September 23, 2019.

134 *It doesn't really hurt to ask for something*
India Today, 'Satvik Hegde Who Clicked a Selfie with PM Modi – Donald
Trump Speaks to *India Today*,' YouTube, September 25, 2019.

135 *I was hesitant at first but then*
Zaidi T, 'Meet Shantanu Naidu, Ratan Tata's Assistant Who Calls Him
"Millennial Dumbledore",' *Business Today*, January 14, 2022.

135 *Shantanu is now a deputy general manager*
Naidu S, '*I Came upon a Lighthouse: A Short Memoir of Life with Ratan Tata*,'
Harper Collins, January 2022.

135 *As a kid, Steve Jobs wanted to build*
Economy P, 'Steve Jobs on the Remarkable Power of Asking for Help,' *Inc.*, 2015.

136 *I've always found something to be very true*
Ibid.

136 *As the saying goes: if you don't ask*
Barstow D, 'If You Don't Ask, the Answer Is Always No: Should We Get Our
Love Advice from Nora Roberts?' *Psychology Today*, June 29, 2018.

136   **After watching Ranbir Kapoor in Tamasha**
Ali I, director, '*Tamasha*,' UTV Motion Picture, 2015.

137   **In 2007, Fortune Small Business magazine**
'America's Best Colleges for Entrepreneurs – Top Professors: Fortune Small Business,' CNN Money, September 2007.
https://money.cnn.com/magazines/fsb/bestcolleges/2007/professors/
(Accessed: July 11, 2022).
'Saras D. Sarasvathy,' Darden School of Business, University of Virginia.
https://www.darden.virginia.edu/faculty-research/directory/saras-d-sarasvathy
(Accessed: July 11, 2022).

137   **In her PhD thesis, Saras tried to understand**
Sarasvathy SD. *'Effectuation: Elements of Entrepreneurial Expertise,'* Edward Elgar Publishing, 2009.

137   **Saras called this 'effectual thinking'**
Sarasvathy SD, 'What Makes Entrepreneurs Entrepreneurial?' 'University of Virginia Darden School Foundation, 2005.

139   **Teaching entrepreneurship is like teaching music**
Rao M, 'The Future Is Not Out There to Be Found. Your Job Is to Make It: Prof. Saras Saraswathy, University of Virginia,' YourStory, February 4, 2014.

139   **Anshu featured in internal brand videos**
'Tamasha: A Journey from IT to Stand-Up,' BITS Embryo, July 14, 2018.

139   **Anshu became friends with Amit Tandon**
Rujvi, 'Anshu Mor, Who Left His Corporate Life and Became One of the Fastest Growing Comedians in India,' *Medium*, July 11, 2017.

139   **Strangely I was not insecure about the move**
Ibid.

140   **To think like an entrepreneur, ask yourself**
Sarasvathy SD. *'Effectuation: Elements of Entrepreneurial Expertise,'* Edward Elgar Publishing, 2009.

141   **Alberto 'Beto' Perez was born in Cali**
Ferreira L, 'Zumba: How a Missing Tape Launched a Global Craze,' BBC, August 12, 2019.

141   **I started to improvise, and people started**
Umoh R, 'How a Mistake at Age 16 Led the Founder of Zumba to Launch a Multimillion-Dollar Business,' CNBC, September 27, 2017.

142   **The two Albertos persuaded Beto**
'Zumba Co-Founder Beto Perez Is Inspiring Others to Follow Their Dreams,' *Modern Wellness Guide*, n.d.

142   *As you start your career*
Ibid.

142   *Zumba is now a global phenomenon*
'Zumba Dances to the Bank on Bollywood Numbers,' *Hindu Business Line*,
March 29, 2017.

142   *During the session he used the track 'Chittiyan Kaliyan'*
Ganesan R, 'Zumba: Beto Perez's Accidental Discovery,' *Business Standard*,
February 7, 2015.

143   *In a survey of Inc. 500 founders*
Bartlett S, Seat of the Pants, *Inc.*, October 15, 2002.

143   *Now let's follow how Marcus Samuelsson's*
Hope NGO, 'Why Marcus Samuelsson Says Cooking Is about Identity,'
Mashed, November 13, 2021.

143   *In* Yes Chef: A Memoir, *Marcus describes*
Samuelsson M and Chambers V, *'Yes, Chef: A Memoir,'* Penguin Random
House, 2012.

144   *In 2010, the Obama administration*
Swarns RL, 'Modern Flourishes at Obamas' State Dinner,' *New York Times*,
November 24, 2009.

144   *Marcus was selected to curate*
Susannah P, 'What's Cooking at the White House? Chef Samuelsson knows...'
Cable News Network, May 26, 2010.

144   *In* The Medici Effect, *Frans Johannsson*
Johansson F, *'The Medici Effect: Breakthrough Insights at the Intersection of Ideas,
Concepts, and Cultures,'* Harvard Business School Press, 2004.

144   *I have had a long-lasting love affair*
Samuelsson M, 'Yes, Chef: Recipes from a Tasty Journey,' Huffington Post Blog,
July 24, 2012.

145   *A study on obesity by Yale University professor*
Christakis NA and Fowler JH, 'The Spread of Obesity in a Large Social
Network over 32 Years,' *New England Journal of Medicine* 357(4), 2007,
370-379.

145   *Mark interviewed people who had switched jobs*
Granovetter MS, 'The Strength of Weak Ties,' *American Journal of Sociology*
78(6), 1973, 1360-1380.

145   *There is a lesson we can learn*
Saxenian A, *'The New Argonauts: Regional Advantage in a Global Economy,'*
Harvard University Press, 2007.

146   What we see in Silicon Valley
Ibid.

147   Is there something wrong with me
Anecdotes on Neha Kirpal are from the following sources:
Sethi S, 'Lunch with BS: Neha Kirpal,' *Business Standard*, January 22, 2016.
Goel P, 'Putting Indian Art on World Map – Neha Kirpal,' YourStory, February 27, 2015.
'Neha Kirpal, 40 Under 40,' *Fortune India*, 2015.
'India Art Fair,' Wikiwand, 2018.
https://www.wikiwand.com/en/India_Art_Fair
(Accessed: August 11, 2022).

148   Business plans are important
'Neha Kirpal, Founder and Fair Director at India Art Fair on What Drove Her into Art,' *Business Today*, September 9, 2014.

148   In 2018, Neha sold her stake in IAF
Spence R, 'Delhi's New-Look India Art Fair,' *Financial Times*, February 16, 2018.

150   Karan Bajaj is the protagonist of all four
Anecdotes on Karan Bajaj are from the following sources:
Bansal S, 'Karan Bajaj: A Winning Discovery,' *Mint*, December 23, 2007.
Janardhan A, 'Karan Bajaj: Cracking the Code,' *Mint,* October 9, 2020.
Singh M, 'India's Byju's Acquires WhiteHat Jr. for $300 Million,' *Tech Crunch*, August 5, 2020.

150   I had actually taken all my savings and spent it
'The Unconventional Journey of Karan Bajaj, Founder, WhiteHat Jr,' *100x Entrepreneur*, May 16, 2021.

151   You play the slots every day
Ibid.

151   Imagine you are the pilot of US Airways Flight 1549
Anecdotes on the 'Miracle on the Hudson' are from the following sources:
Langewiesche W, 'Anatomy of a Miracle,' *Vanity Fair*, May 5, 2009.
Smith A, 'The Miracle on the Hudson: How It Happened,' *The Telegraph*, November 22, 2016.
John AS, 'What Went Right: Revisiting Captain "Sully" Sullenberger and the Miracle on the Hudson,' *Popular Mechanics*, January 15, 2019.

152   We're going to be in the Hudson
Associated Press, 'Pilot: We're Going to Be in the Hudson,' YouTube, February 5, 2009.

152   No one warned us
Eastwood C, director, '*Sully: Miracle on the Hudson,*' Warner Bros Pictures, 2016.

Patni P, 'The Last Mile Heroes,' LinkedIn, January 7, 2017.
https://www.linkedin.com/pulse/last-mile-heroes-pallav-patni/
(Accessed: June 1, 2022).

153   Shradha Sharma is from Patna
Sharma S, 'Congratulations! You Lack What It Takes,' Linkedin, October 2, 2015.
https://www.linkedin.com/pulse/congratulations-you-lack-what-takes-shradha-sharma/
(Accessed: June 1, 2022).

154   Whatever you did not get
INK Talks, 'Shradha Sharma: What You Lack, Will Make You Run,' YouTube,
November 14, 2016.

154   Shradha founded YourStory, an online platform
'Shradha Sharma: At a Glance,' *Forbes India*, 2018.
UpGrad, 'Entrepreneur Speak, YourStory's Founder - Shradha Sharma on
Entrepreneurship,' YouTube, April 12, 2017.

154   It's not that I wanted to run a business
Josh Talks, 'How to Succeed as a Woman Entrepreneur? Shradha Sharma,
YourStory,' YouTube, August 10, 2015.

154   YourStory received angel funding
'Ratan Tata Reads YourStory, and Writes a Cheque for It,' *Business Standard*,
August 18, 2015.

The Toolkit

158   Men wanted for hazardous journey
Anecdotes on Shackleton and 'Endurance' are from the following sources:
'The Great Survivor: Ernest Shackleton,' *Time*, September 12, 2003.
'Shackleton's Voyage of Endurance: Diary of a Survivor,' PBS, April 11, 1916.
Mulvaney K, 'The Stunning Survival Story of Ernest Shackleton and His
Endurance Crew,' March 9, 2022.
https://www.history.com/news/shackleton-endurance-survival
(Accessed: July 12, 2022).

159   Ship and stores have gone, so now we'll go
Shea GP, 'Leading in Hard Times: Lessons from Shackleton,' Centre for
Leadership and Change Management, Wharton, University of Pennsylvania.
https://leadershipcenter.wharton.upenn.edu/education/leading-in-hard-times-lessons-from-shackleton/
(Accessed: July 12, 2022).

160   Shackleton had a goal
Koehn NF, 'Leadership Lessons from the Shackleton Expedition,' *New York
Times*, December 24, 2011.

160   ***A Business Model Ca.ivas (BMC) is a strategic tool***
Osterwalder A, 'A Better Way to Think about Your Business Model,' *Harvard Business Review*, May 6, 2013.
https://hbr.org/2013/05/a-better-way-to-think-about-yo
(Accessed: August 12, 2022).

162   ***In the Japanese concept of 'ikigai'***
Garcia H and Miralles F, *'Ikigai: The Japanese Secret to a Long and Happy Life,'* Penguin Life, 2017.

162   ***Your goals should be SMART***
Doran GT, 'There's a SMART Way to Write Management's Goals and Objectives,' *Management Review* 70(11),1981, 35-36.

163   ***The Temple of Apollo in Delphi***
Best K, 'Know Thyself: The Philosophy of Self-Knowledge,' University of Connecticut, August 2018.

164   ***Did you know that the game of snakes and ladders***
Rao VV, 'Who Invented the Board Game Snakes and Ladders?' *Times Of India*, October 12, 2008.

164   ***How do you seek opportunities in a VUCA***
Bennet N and Lemoine GJ, 'What VUCA Really Means for You,' *Harvard Business Review* 92(1-2), 2014, 27.

165   ***Have you heard of Chaturanga***
Mitra A, 'International Chess Day: Tracing the Game's Indian Roots and Its Gradual Evolution,' *Reader's Digest*, July 20, 2020.

Epilogue

167   ***At any given age, you're getting better***
Karlgaard R, *'Late Bloomers: The Power of Patience in a World Obsessed with Early Achievement,'* Penguin Random House, 2019.

167   ***Richard studied at Stanford University***
Anecdote on Richard Karlgaard is from the following sources:
Hamilton D, 'The Case for Late Bloomers with Rich Karlgaard,' Dr. Diane Hamilton, 2020.
Fisher LM, 'Making a Difference; Another Side to Upside,' *New York Times*. April 12, 1992.
Karlgaard R, 'Stepping Down & Up,' *Forbes ASAP*, 162(4), August 28, 1998.
https://www.forbes.com/asap/1998/0824/011.html.
(Accessed: Sept 7, 2022).

168   ***Life 2.0, published in 2004***
Karlgaard R, *'Life 2.0: How People across America are Transforming Their Lives by Finding the Where of Their Happiness,'* Crown Business, 2004.

168 *Sociologists describe this as*
Henig RM, 'What Is It About 20-Somethings?' *New York Times*, August 18, 2010.

168 *Film Director Satyajit Ray was 34*
Bhambri N, 'Satyajit Ray: An Auteur of the Highest Order,' *Khabar Magazine*, September 2021.

168 *It won 11 international awards*
'Satyajit Ray: The Lesser-Known Facts about the First Indian to Win Honorary Oscar,' News 18, April 23, 2019.

168 *At 54, he wrote his first book*
Chaudhuri NC, *'The Autobiography of an Unknown Indian,'* University of California Press, 1951.

168 *Fauja Singh began running marathons*
Conn J, 'The Runner: Fauja Singh Ran His First Marathon at Age 89 and Became an International Sensation,' ESPN, February 22, 2013.

168 *He clocked his best time of six hours*
Press Trust of India, 'Marathon Man Fauja Singh Does It Again in Dubai,' *Times of India*, November 8, 2011.

INDEX

ACKNOWLEDGEMENTS

Schitt's Creek, a Canadian television sitcom, enjoys a cult following and has won numerous awards. It's about the Rose family who were once millionaires before their business manager embezzled their fortune. The parents and their grown-up children move to the eponymous small town that they had once purchased as a joke. The family adapts and later learns to thrive in their new environment.

The story was created by Eugene and Dan Levy, who play father and son and are also so in real life. At the end of 80 episodes over six seasons, Dan had this message for his fans:

> *I don't think there has been a single day over the past*
> *seven years when I have not thought about the show.*
> *Is that taxing?*
> *No.*
> *But it is all-consuming.*

We share that thought, with one exception.
It was taxing.

* * *

We (Mukesh and Priyank) met for the first time on a wintery morning in 2015, on the lawns of the Centre for Innovation and Incubation (CIIE) at IIM Ahmedabad (IIMA). Sanjeev Bikhchandani, an alumnus of IIMA and founder of Ashoka University, was the catalyst in getting the two institutions to collaborate. Our next pit stop was Ashish Dhawan's home in Delhi. Over tea and vegan cake, Pramath Raj Sinha and Vineet Gupta helped crystallize the collaboration. Leadership at IIMA, including Ashish Nanda and Errol D'Souza, who were respectively director and dean at that time, supported this adventure. With well-wishers like them on board, we just needed to make sure that we did not mess things up.

Our journey with *Leapfrog* was serendipitous. Over conversations at the Ashoka University cafeteria, we wondered why many concepts and theories, widely known in the social sciences, remain tucked away in scholarly journals. As our students embarked on their careers, might they benefit from these practices and even use them at work?

As we bounced these ideas off colleagues, students, and alumni, it became evident that we needed to write a book. In academia, we often joke that when you want to learn about a subject, offer a course on it. In our case, it was the book.

Medha Agrawal, then a teaching assistant at Ashoka University, and Pooja Srivastav, our student, were our first collaborators. We bounced ideas off them, got them to read articles, books, and research papers on topics we wanted to learn about. We imagined them as our first potential readers.

To learn about scholarly research in other disciplines, we began conversations with colleagues at both IIMA and Ashoka University. They included Amit Karna, Saikat Majumdar, Ankur Sarin, Asha Kaul, Biju Varkkey, Chinmay Tumbe, Devasmita

Chakraverty, Jeevant Rampal, Pawan Mamidi, Satish Deodhar, Sunil Sharma, and many others.

The first and last names in that list—Amit and Sunil—were a source of inspiration and later needled us to complete what we had begun. Witness to constant delays, Amit once enquired whether we were on our second or third book, or maybe even a new volume of the original. Sunil maintained a scholarly and studious silence.

We had an opportunity to move the project forward while travelling to the Academy of Management conference in August 2019. The Dubai to Boston leg was spent at the rear of the aircraft in the Emirates sky lounge. The tempting choice of exotic drinks at the bar was foregone for a bigger cause.

An initial draft of the chapters was read by Alisha Aranha, who made useful suggestions. We then worked with Madhuri Dempsey, who helped us develop this manuscript in creative ways. The story of Marie Kondo, and many others, came from hours of brainstorming together. With her patience, professionalism, and eye for detail, Madhuri also mentored us on the rules of grammar followed in publishing. It sometimes felt like being in school and reading *Wren & Martin* again.

The images and illustrations were a potpourri from several sources. We worked with Dharun Vyas from the Fingerprint Collective team, and later with Vagmi Karera and Meghana Walimbe. They encouraged us to be quirky and a little irreverent in the book's feel and style. Many others contributed to the illustrations, including Sumantra Mukherjee and Sayan Mukherjee. No, they are not related.

With the novel ideas we would be writing about, we needed to give our readers detailed references. Sachin Arya and Advaita Rajendran helped in compiling the notes and reference section. We couldn't have put this together without the support of the reference team at the Vikram Sarabhai Library at IIMA.

This book is dedicated to our students. While many of them contributed to the stories, some came forth with incredible ideas and anecdotes. Thanks to Deepain Yadav, Kavya Satish, Naman Bhatnagar, Ridhima Manocha, Ritvik Sharma, Rohin Mukherjee, Shivani Bajaj, and Yashraj Nanda. Arnav Mohan Gupta connected us with amazing people in his network. Ujwal Kalra, despite being busy writing his own book and launching a company, was always an enthusiastic supporter.

In addition, our teams at Ashoka and IIMA—Arushi Tandon, Ekanto Ghosh, Manoj Dinne, Sagar Singhal, Shoeb Chobdar, and many others—were with us on this journey. Samarth Kholkar, Vidushi Malhotra, and Vir Kapoor shared their personal stories with us.

The team at Penguin Random House have been true collaborators. We were fortunate to connect with Sanjiv Gupta, a stalwart of publishing. Having an editor like Premanka Goswami can be a game changer for any writer. It was for us. He guided us with patience and a smile while Binita Roy supported us tirelessly through many rounds of edits. Ahlawat Gunjan did an excellent job with the cover and layout. A special word of appreciation for Karthik Venkatesh, Joginder Singh, Harish Papnai, and Nazaqat Ahamed for their support to this project.

It is said that it takes a village to raise a child; this is so true about our book.

—**Mukesh and Priyank**